Foreword

Diversity is the basis of biological survival. Each of us has a particular genetic structure; unique facial features; a distinguishing thumbprint; a distinctive signature; a background of knowledge, experience, and culture; and a preferred way of gathering, processing, and expressing information and knowledge. We even have our singular frequencies in which we vibrate. George Leonard (1986) observes that all living things are oscillators: "The simplest single-celled organism oscillates to a number of different frequencies, at the atomic, molecular, sub-cellular, and cellular levels; microscopic movies of these organisms are striking for the ceaseless, rhythmic pulsation that is revealed. In an organism as complex as a human being, the frequencies of oscillation and the interactions between those frequencies are multitudinous."

Life would be simpler if everybody were similar, but the truth is that all people, deep within their genetic and bodily drives, yearn and strive to exert their individualism. Embedded in many educational practices, however, are policies and procedures that lead individuals toward uniformity: grading on a curve, I.Q. tests, curriculum guides, textbook adoptions, standardized achievement tests, criteria for judging excellence, grade-level demarcation, Carnegie Units, and so forth.

Perhaps Winston Churchill (1987) best illustrates the point:

> I had scarcely passed my 12th birthday when I entered the inhospitable regions of examinations, through which for the next seven years, I was destined to journey. These examinations were a great trial to me. The subjects which were dearest to the examiners were almost invariably those I fancied least. I would have liked to have been examined in history, poetry, and writing essays. The examiners, on the other hand were partial to Latin and mathematics. And their will prevailed. Moreover, the questions which they asked on both these subjects were almost invariably those to which I was unable to suggest the satisfactory answer. I should have liked to be asked to say what I know. They always tried to ask what I did not know. When I would willingly have displayed my knowledge, they sought to expose my ignorance. This sort of treatment had only one result, I did not do well in examinations.

I have a close friend whose daughter is dyslexic. The daughter has always had difficulty in school and is invariably enrolled in special education classes. Last year, California State University, Sacramento, awarded her a music scholarship. She plays cello in their symphony orchestra. The "perfect 10" Olympic gold medal diver Greg Louganis was never as adept at learning in school as he is at diving. British Prime Minister John Majors was a high school dropout. Winston Churchill was thought to be retarded because he frequently played with toy soldiers when he was young. Eleanor Roosevelt, Albert Einstein, and numerous other notables were deemed "retarded," "slow," "handicapped," or "disturbed" learners.

As educators, we've known only too well the class clown who keeps us in stitches with puns and anecdotes but flunks math tests. We've marveled at those social magnets to whom other students cling but who are not good in spelling. We've seen students who cannot express themselves in writing but who, when provided with crayons, paints, or clay, can communicate their ideas with great clarity.

Because public education favors a narrow range of verbal and visual intelligence, we miss those more elusive qualities of humanness. The industrial era influenced our picture of education, schooling, and intelligence. When we counted the number of items produced as a measure of work done, workers' efficiency and ability were reduced to numbers. As the Irish social commentator George W. Russell stated, "When steam first began to pump and wheels go round at so many revolutions per minute, what are called business habits were intended to make the life of man run in harmony with the steam engine, and his movement rival the train in punctuality." Educators, influenced by the time-management experts, also viewed student learning capacities numerically. Lord Kelvin is quoted as saying, "If you cannot measure it, if you cannot reduce it to numbers, your knowledge is of a meager and unsatisfactory kind." Thus evolved our image of intelligence as a static numerical score—132, 70, 100—for which we were forever cursed or blessed. Our view of human greatness was counted, summed, and reduced to digits.

In the midst of the postindustrial era, however, we are increasingly cognizant of human potential as our greatest natural resource. Valuing a range of diverse skills and capacities makes a business, a community, a society, and a nation strong. We are realizing that collaboratively drawing on the resources of diversity gives a product, an idea, or a plan greater potential and power. And Howard Gardner's theory of multiple intelligences has not only expanded our list of unique qualities, but also revolutionized our concept of human capacity.

On a recent flight from Chicago to Honolulu, I sat next to a pilot who flies 747s for United Airlines. While he would have much preferred to have been on the flight deck, I was able to engage him in some

SEVEN PATHWAYS
OF LEARNING

SEVEN PATHWAYS
OF LEARNING

*Teaching Students and Parents
about Multiple Intelligences*

DAVID LAZEAR

Foreword by Arthur L. Costa

Zephyr Press

Tucson, Arizona

Seven Pathways of Learning
Teaching Students and Parents about Multiple Intelligences

Grades: All ages

© 1994 by Zephyr Press
Printed in the United States of America

ISBN 0-913705-92-6

Editors: Stacey Lynn and Stacey Shropshire
Design and production: Nancy Taylor
Cover art and design: David Fischer
Book illustrations: John Reedy

Zephyr Press
P.O. Box 66006
Tucson, Arizona 85728-6006

Library of Congress Cataloging-in-Publication Data

Lazear, David G.
    Seven pathways to learning : teaching students and parents about
multiple intelligences / David Lazear.
        p. cm.
    ISBN 0-913705-92-6
    1. Learning.   2. Intellect.   3. Cognitive styles.   4. Teaching.
5. Activity programs in education.   I. Title.   II. Title: 7
pathways to learning.   III. Title: Multiple intelligences.
LB1060.L387 1993
370.15'23—dc20   93-33054

Printed on recycled paper

It is of the utmost importance that we recognize and nurture all of the varied human intelligences, and all of the combinations of intelligences. . . . If we can mobilize the spectrum of human abilities, not only will people feel better about themselves and more competent; it is even possible that they will also feel more engaged and better able to join the rest of the world community in working for the broader good. Perhaps if we can mobilize the full range of human intelligences and ally them to an ethical sense, we can help to increase the likelihood of our survival on this planet, and perhaps even contribute to our thriving.

—Howard Gardner

Contents

CONTENTS

intriguing conversation. I inquired as to the nature of pilots' training and the rigor required to advance to the status of captain. "Does anyone ever get washed out?" I inquired. "Oh, yes," was his reply. "Just recently, I served on an examination team for a flight engineer who was requesting advancement to second officer. He didn't make it. Part of the examination that United puts us through," he explained, "is a simulation of an in-flight crisis situation. This person did not call upon the resources of the other members of his flight deck team to assist in solving the problem. He thought he could solve the problem all by himself. He was washed out!" This anecdote is indicative of a situation unique to our modern life of complex problem solving. No one person can have all the answers to all the problems. Knowing how to network, how to draw on diverse resources, and how to value others' expertise, views, perceptions, and knowledge is essential to survival. We might view these skills as a new form of interlocking intelligences: collaboratively melding the perceptions, modalities, skills, capacities, and expertise into a unified whole that is better and more efficient than any one of its parts.

Furthermore, people whom we deem most effective seem at home in many areas of functioning. They move flexibly from one style to another as the situation demands it. They have an uncanny ability to read clues from the situation or the environment to determine what is needed. They bring forward from their vast repertoire those skills and capacities needed to function most effectively in any setting.

Music educator Joseph O'Conner and organizational consultant and trainer John Seymour (1990) report that "no system is better in an absolute sense than another; it depends what you want to do. Athletes need a well-developed kinesthetic awareness, and it is difficult to be a successful architect without a facility for making clear, constructed mental pictures. One skill shared by outstanding performers in any field is to be able to move easily through all the representational systems and use the most appropriate one for the task at hand."

It is to the development of more effectively functioning human beings that David Lazear has dedicated his work. His Seven Ways handbooks serve educators and parents in helping students to become aware of and to manage the multiplicity of their own and others' unique forms of intelligence; in knowing how and when to employ and evaluate the usefulness of each intelligence; and in respecting other people's preferences for and levels of intellectual development. Lazear's work also illuminates a vision of an educational community in which each member's range of multiple intelligence capacities is maximally developed.

To adopt this new vision, educators will need to be prepared to "get off the digm"—to experience a paradigm shift. Some of our traditional ways of viewing education, learning, teaching, achievement, and talent will be found to be obsolescent and will demand to be replaced with more modern and relevant policies, practices, and philosophies. As our paradigm shifts, for example, we will need to let go of our obsession with acquiring content and knowledge as an end in itself and make room for viewing content as a vehicle for developing various forms of intelligence; we will dismiss uniformity in deference to valuing diversity; we will give up external evaluation of students in favor of students' self-examination; we will devalue competition and enhance interdependence; we will redefine *smart* to mean having a repertoire of intelligences and knowing when to use each.

Jean Houston's (1987) comment "Never has the vision of what human beings can be been more remarkable" becomes even more profound as we more clearly envision, more stridently demand, and more eagerly install those educational and societal conditions in which humanness is enhanced. The fullest development of the intellects today will allow our students and all the world's citizens to continue developing future visions of ever more remarkable human beings.

This book provides a pathway to that future.

Arthur L. Costa, Ed.D.
Professor Emeritus
California State University
Sacramento, California

Preface

This is my third book on the seven intelligences. The first, *Seven Ways of Knowing,* is about teaching *for* multiple intelligences. It focuses on integrating the various intelligence capacities and skills into existing school curricula. The message of this first book is that, if we want our children to be as intelligent as they can be on as many levels as possible, then we must teach the specific skills for using each intelligence in developmentally appropriate ways. This approach takes students on a journey of exploration that moves from the attainment of the basic skills of each intelligence through students' more complex development for acquiring knowledge and processing information. The approach leads them through the higher-order use of the intelligences to solve problems and meet daily challenges, culminating in a variety of vocational and avocational pursuits.

The topic of the second book, *Seven Ways of Teaching,* is teaching *with* multiple intelligences. The second book's focus is the revitalization of classroom instruction using the seven ways of knowing. The book presents seven full-blown lessons (one for each intelligence) to use in traditional academic areas such as history, math, science and health, language arts, social studies, the practical arts, and the fine arts. It presents a dynamic, four-stage model for designing lessons. Stage one awakens various intelligences in students, stage two gives them an opportunity to practice particular intelligence skills, and stage three utilizes those skills in a content-based lesson. The final stage of the model provides ideas for appropriate assessment and helps students transfer their learning of a given lesson beyond the classroom.

This book, *Seven Pathways of Learning,* is devoted to teaching *about* multiple intelligences and thus presents the metacognitive dimension of this work. *Seven Pathways* is concerned with reinventing the learning process from a multiple intelligence perspective. This book describes ways to expand intelligent behavior, whether in school or in other everyday situations outside of the classroom, in an endeavor to give teachers the means for relating multiple intelligence theory and practice to students and parents.

I dedicate this book to the hundreds of teachers, principals, and administrators who are actively working to incorporate teaching for, with, and about multiple intelligences into the typical school and classroom situation. These educators are truly the pioneers of an important new trend that is moving across the United States and Canada, changing the paradigm of education. In the last two or three years I have had the privilege of getting to know and working with many of these people in and through various professional development workshops. I believe the ways in which they are applying this paradigm are on the cutting edge of the next phase of multiple intelligence research. Those people I mention here are representative of hundreds of others who are similarly concerned.

Dr. Yolanda Rey, Superintendent for Curriculum and Instruction, El Paso Independent School District, El Paso, Texas, and Lorene Patneaude, Director of Staff Development, El Paso Independent School District, are pioneers in introducing multiple intelligences on a district-wide basis. They have made it possible for more than five hundred teachers within the district to receive basic training in teaching for multiple intelligences. Some one hundred fifty of these teachers have received advanced training in restructuring daily lessons with multiple intelligences and in working with the metacognitive aspects of teaching students about the multiple ways of knowing in school. The district has also created an in-district cadre of multiple intelligence trainers.

The Governor Bent Elementary School in Albuquerque, New Mexico, has completely restructured itself based on multiple intelligences. This school, led by principal Marilyn Davenport, is a wonderful model of a thoroughly integrated approach to dealing with multiple intelligences in and through daily classroom instruction.

The Elk Elementary Center, Charleston, West Virginia, a new elementary education center, has made teaching for, with, and about multiple intelligences part of what is expected in the school. Principal Leonard Allen and the staff have made multiple intelligences a regular part of the teacher evaluation process. The school also provides special awareness training for parents to help them understand the "MI approach" to school more fully. In the coming years, Elk Center will experiment with new models for assessment that are based on multiple intelligences.

Patricia Steele, Indiana principal of the year in 1992, has led her staff at the Kingsbury Elementary School on an exciting restructuring journey based on the theme of creating an "enrichment-based curriculum." Multiple intelligence theory is at the core of their restructuring efforts, which include curriculum integration using the intelligences as the integrating principle and regular implementation of MI lesson planning and teaching strategies. Plans for using alternate, authentic, multiple intelligence–based assessment practices are currently in process.

Kahale Kukea, principal of the prestigious Kamehameha Elementary School in Honolulu, Hawaii, is in the process of a dramatic curriculum restructuring effort based on multiple intelligence theory. I have had the privilege of working with many of the Kamehameha teachers in their classrooms, as well as in multiple intelligence training workshops. A number of the ideas and model lessons in this book were first piloted with students in the classrooms of the Kamehameha Elementary School.

Two professional organizations are doing a great deal to get the good news about multiple intelligences out to educators around the world. Phi Delta Kappa has used me as a presenter in various professional development institutes and has published my Fastback pamphlet that deals with multiple intelligences. This relationship has provided me with an opportunity to communicate with many educators across the United States and Canada about the implications of multiple intelligences for school restructuring today.

I also thank the Association for Supervision and Curriculum Development (ASCD) for their sponsorship and support of the member-initiated Teaching for Multiple Intelligences Network, of which I am the facilitator. The network has provided a forum for many teachers and principals to share practical applications of the theory of multiple intelligences to daily situations in school and classroom, and it has assisted in spreading the word about what is possible when we find ways to help students discover their full intellectual potential by moving beyond traditional approaches to education.

I must also again thank Howard Gardner, the father of the theory of multiple intelligences, for his continued support, feedback, advice, and encouragement in completing all of my books on the multiple intelligences.

To all of you who have made my life so rich and so full in the last few years as I have been working on these three books, thank you. None of the books would have been possible without your prodding, feedback, and support.

David G. Lazear
New Dimensions of Learning
Chicago, 1993

Introduction
Meta-Intelligence

HELPING STUDENTS TAP THEIR FULL LEARNING POTENTIAL IN SCHOOL

In a school that is a home for the mind there is an inherent faith that all people can continue to improve their intellectual capacities throughout life; that learning to think is as valid a goal for the "at risk," the handicapped, the disadvantaged, and the foreign-speaking as it is for the "gifted and talented"; and that all of us have the potential for even greater creativity and intellectual power.

ART COSTA, *THE SCHOOL AS A HOME FOR THE MIND*

As far as we know, human beings are the only creatures that possess the ability to be self-reflective; that is, we have the ability to step back from ourselves and watch ourselves, almost like outside observers. This capacity carries with it both the joy of freedom and the burden of responsibility. We are not victims. Once we become aware of something in our lives, our self-consciousness gives us the power to change it, if we so desire. This self-reflective dimension is at the heart of helping students understand their own multiple intelligences, how to improve those intelligences, and how to use them consciously to enhance the students' own and others' lives.

The cognitive research of the last ten to fifteen years overwhelmingly supports the necessity and possibility of teaching students how to increase their skills of knowing, understanding, perceiving, and learning. In his article "Thinking Skills: Neither an Add-On nor a Quick-Fix," Art Costa (1991) makes the following observation:

> For many years we thought that thinking skills programs were intended to challenge the intellectually gifted. Indeed, some thought that any child whose I.Q. fell below a certain static score was forever doomed to remedial or compensatory drill and practice.
>
> Gaining wide acceptance, four fundamental and refreshing concepts underlie modern cognitive curriculum and instructional practices. They are: The Theory of Cognitive Modifiability (Feuerstein 1980), the Theory of Multiple Intelligences (Gardner 1983), the faith that Intelligence Can Be Taught (Whimbley 1975), and Sternberg's thesis that traditional I.Q. scores have very little to do with success in dealing with the problems encountered in daily life (Hammer 1985; McKean 1985).
>
> These theoretical concepts equip us with the realization that *all* human beings are both retarded in certain problem-solving skills, while simultaneously being gifted in others (Link, as quoted in Makler 1980). The concepts provide us the faith that *all* human beings can continue to develop their intelligent behavior throughout a lifetime.

Seven Pathways of Learning is about helping all of our students continue to develop their intelligent behavior and their intellectual capacities throughout their lifetimes. I like to call this kind of teaching and learning "meta-intelligence," adapting the idea of metacognition to working with the seven ways of knowing. Stop for a moment and answer the following questions:

- Do you talk to yourself? What do you talk to yourself about?
- Do you answer yourself? Are you often your own best therapist?
- Why do you go through this process? What benefits do you get from it?

Don't worry—talking to yourself is probably not early senility setting in. It's metacognitive behavior! In his article "Mediating the Metacognitive" Art Costa (1984) calls the process of metacognition "inner talking": " Occurring in the neocortex and therefore thought by some neurologists to be uniquely human, metacognition is our ability to know what we know and what we don't know. It is our ability to plan a strategy for producing what information is needed, to be conscious of our own steps and strategies during the act of problem solving, and to reflect on and evaluate the productiveness of our own thinking." The process of teaching about multiple intelligences, meta-intelligence, is simply intelligence investigating and thinking about itself.

Current research on metacognition documents four distinct levels of information processing, with each level becoming more meta-cognitively sophisticated than the previous one. I have structured this book around these levels and have adapted them to the task of helping students and parents become more aware of the seven ways of knowing, learn how to use them effectively to be more successful in school, and acquire a full repertoire of intelligence tools and skills for dealing with the task of daily living beyond the classroom. The lessons, or intelligence learning activities, presented in this book are an attempt to catalyze more intelligences in the classroom and to help students transfer the use of the full spectrum of their intellectual potentials to everyday life.[1]

LEVEL 1: TACIT INTELLIGENCE

The tacit level of teaching and learning about multiple intelligences involves helping students become aware of capacities and potentials that we generally take for granted. We do many "intelligent" things each day without realizing how really clever we are. Think about what is involved in crossing the street without getting hit by an automobile, listening to music to relax at the end of a day, making a grocery list, parallel parking, drawing diagrams or maps to help someone get from one place to another, using body language to communicate feelings and ideas, telling and understanding jokes, and balancing a checkbook. The tacit level for teaching and learning about the seven ways of knowing involves activities to help students become aware of the capacities and potentials that are the students' legacy as part of the human species and to help them recognize these capacities as intelligent behavior.

I use the seven intelligences every day; I've just never called them that!

1. The following description of the levels is adapted with permission from the PDK Fastback series.

LEVEL 2: AWARE INTELLIGENCE

Now that I have labels for the various ways of knowing, I can practice them and make them stronger.

The aware level of teaching and learning about multiple intelligences involves learning about the neurobiology of the intelligences and how we can improve their functioning. Once we can name the intelligent behaviors we use during the day, it is possible for us to work on strengthening and expanding our "intelligence functioning." In many ways, the intelligences are like any skill we possess—the more we practice them, the better we become at using them.

The aware level involves two tasks: (1) learning how each of the intelligences operates in the brain/mind/body system, and (2) evaluating one's own relative strengths and weaknesses in the various intelligence areas. Once we have done these tasks, we can become conscious participants in our own intellectual development. If some students discover that they are not very good at using the active imagination (a visual/spatial intelligence capacity), for example, they should also be told about or shown exercises and activities they can use to improve or strengthen this capacity within themselves.

LEVEL 3: STRATEGIC INTELLIGENCE

Not only do I know about the seven intelligences, but I know when and how to use each one most effectively.

The strategic level of teaching and learning about the seven ways of knowing encompasses the two previous levels of meta-intelligence but adds the conscious decision to employ the seven intelligences regularly to enhance learning, expand creativity, and improve problem-solving abilities. Students suddenly realize that they have many tools in their "kitbags" to help them know, understand, perceive, and learn. For example, if one student is assisting another with schoolwork, the helper may be able to "translate" a lesson into a preferred or stronger intelligence modality for the other student. Or a student might consciously use a variety of ways to solve a problem, including drawing, talking with others, acting it out, thinking about it, or trying to visualize a solution. In other words, the strategic use of the intelligences is using them with intention.

LEVEL 4: REFLECTIVE INTELLIGENCE

I am learning how to use all seven ways of knowing to help me in my daily life.

The reflective level of teaching and learning about the intelligences involves activities that help students integrate the seven ways of knowing into daily life. Students can use the seven intelligences to approach any problem, challenge, project, or goal. What is more, when we "cook on more burners" as we go about the task of daily living, we can access greater levels of creativity and inventiveness within ourselves than if we use only one approach. Likewise, the seven intelligences not only make various learning tasks more fun; they also broaden and deepen our knowledge base, for we know and understand something in at least seven ways, not just one.

Each level of this model represents an increasingly complex understanding of and facility in using the different ways of knowing. Each level also assumes and contains the previous level within an ever-widening spiral of understanding of and skill in using various intelligence capacities.

*Get up out of your seats—
you've been sitting too long!*

TEACHING FOR INTELLIGENT BEHAVIOR IN SCHOOL

One of the major assumptions of this book is that we, as educators, need to do whatever it takes to teach students about their own multiple intelligences. Current cognitive research clearly shows that the more conscious students can become of every dimension of the teaching/learning process, the better they can be and will become as active learners who see themselves as responsible for their own learning. Part of our task is to lead students systematically through the development of the meta-intelligence levels I suggest in this book. You will need to create developmentally appropriate adaptations of the various lessons, activities, and extensions presented in this book.

I have assumed that teachers who use this book already understand the value and importance of teaching their students about the seven ways of knowing and, even more important, that these teachers will find the time to work with students on these meta-intelligence activities. I can confidently say that in 100 percent of typical classroom situations, time spent teaching students *about* multiple intelligences will bear much fruit both in students' academic performance and in their lives beyond the classroom. Second, I can guarantee that teaching *about* multiple intelligences will produce students who are active, eager learners. Is there an educator you know who could ask for anything more?

Yes, initially, some extra classroom time is required to introduce students to the concept that they have seven ways of knowing, not just one. But once students begin to learn how to use their multiple intelligences to be more successful in school and in living, it becomes easier and easier to integrate the "teaching *about*" into your daily classroom lessons, where, I hope, teaching *with* the intelligences is already part of your normal instructional practice (see Lazear 1991).

More talking with your neighbors.

What Is Involved?

What is involved in teaching students about their own multiple ways of knowing so that the students are able to transfer the skills within given subject areas, across the curriculum, and finally into their lives beyond the classroom? Dr. Barry Beyer is one of the key figures involved in the cognitive research of the last ten years. He is the leading advocate for explicitly teaching various thinking skills to students. He calls this approach "the teaching of thinking." In *Patterns for Thinking, Patterns for Transfer*, Robin Fogarty and James Bellanca (1989) summarize Beyer's approach:

Let's try putting this problem to music!

In his approach, the teacher identifies 4–8 thinking skills which are already included in the subject matter. For instance, classification is taught implicitly in biology, problem-solving is implicit in word problems, attributing in character analysis of a novel. Although the best students are able to grasp these thinking skills which are buried in the content, most students seldom recognize or master them. As a result, when they have to use the skills without teacher direction, the students can only guess at what to do. Beyer argues that formal instruction in explicit thinking skills will give all students the tools to do more skillful thinking.

Beyer's argument also holds true for multiple intelligences. If we want students to be intelligent in all seven ways, then we must explicity teach them the skills of using their seven intelligences. What is involved in this kind of formal intelligence instruction? There are three general stages in this task:

Skill Transfer Model of Instruction

1. *Learning basic intelligence skills and capacities.* Research suggests that when teaching students a new skill, we should begin with a situation that is relatively free of content or one in which the content is familiar. This approach gives students the opportunity to focus on the skill or capacity you are trying to teach rather than worrying about something they must know for a test later on.

   - **Intelligence stimulation** (also known as the "hook" or "turning on the brain"). Begin with a fun activity that triggers a particular intelligence in the brain and sparks students' interest. The activity should be related to the particular intelligence skill you will be employing later in the lesson. The best activities for awakening the intelligence are generally games, puzzles, exercises, and other no-stress learning activities (see Lazear 1991).
   - **Explaining lesson goals** (also known as "revealing your teaching secrets"). Students need to know and understand the objective of the lesson. The more they know about and understand the teaching and learning strategies you will be using and why you are using those strategies, the better learners they will become, and you may even find the students will help you teach the lesson!
   - **Amplifying skills** (also known as "intelligence workout" or "skill practice"). When teaching students various intelligence skills, you must first model the skill for them and explain to them what you are doing. Then give them an opportunity to try it out immediately for themselves, again in an environment that is as free of content as possible. This situation is very much "monkey see, monkey do." For example, demonstrate compare-and-contrast thinking by comparing one half of the class to the other, then give students an opportunity to practice the same skill using whatever items they choose.

2. *Practice, practice, and more practice using the skills and capacities in academic content areas.* Once students have learned a basic intelligence skill as described in number 1, you are ready to help them learn how to apply the skill in actual, structured learning tasks. It is best to begin working within a single content area, giving students opportunities to practice the skills and capacities they have learned. Contemporary cognitive research suggests that it takes three or four times of practicing a particular skill, beginning in one subject and then applying it to other subjects, to catalyze the transfer process. For example, teach students the skill of expressing their ideas through role-play, then ask them to apply this skill to learning math concepts, to understanding a period of history, to performing a scientific experiment, or to understanding characters in a novel.

3. *Experiments in utilizing intelligence skills and capacities beyond the classroom.* After students have learned how to use the seven intelligences in school, it is time to encourage them to apply the intelligences outside of the classroom. Assign the students to use their multiple intelligences in dealing with various family, individual, and peer situations, such as planning a family summer vacation, deciding their electives for the next school term, or solving conflicts with friends.

NURTURING INTELLIGENT BEHAVIOR AT HOME

The second major assumption of this book is that there are many relatively simple things parents can do at home to help children stretch their intellectual limits. Parents need to know about multiple intelligences and to learn how to work with their children to develop and use multiple ways of knowing, understanding, perceiving, and learning.

At the end of each chapter in this book is a special section titled "Notes to Parents." These sections, which you can copy and give to parents, are designed not only to give parents a basic understanding of the seven intelligences, but more important, to give them ideas for incorporating the seven ways of knowing into the daily life of the family. I suggest at least three areas through which parents can nurture, and even evoke, a full spectrum of intellectual capacities in their children in and through regular family life. These areas, along with some typical activities, are illustrated below.

Family at Play
- **games**
- **hobbies**
- **theater**
- **TV/movies/videos**
- **outings**

Routine Family Life
- **problems/challenges**
- **mealtimes**
- **planning times**
- **family rules**
- **discussions**

School/Homework
- **test preparation**
- **basic understanding**
- **hard concepts**
- **weak academic areas**
- **boring work**

The notes to parents provide a wide variety of practical activities (for example, games, puzzles, brain teasers, etc.) parents can use in the various dimensions of family life to nurture and promote their children's full intellectual development. These special parents' sections also include basic information on the intelligences, and the sections summarize key aspects of the research that supports developing the intelligences in children.

I believe that parents can be of great help to their own children and their children's teachers. Parents can help children transfer classroom learning (in this case, learning about the intelligences) beyond school, which means, in effect, that not only are children expected to be as intelligent as possible in multiple ways in school, but that we are reinforcing this expectation at home, asking children to use their full intelligence capacities in the family. Parent involvement will also be useful to teachers because it will make every situation a learning situation, which is the key for instilling a passion for lifelong learning in our children.

HOW TO USE THIS BOOK

Chapters 1 through 4 offer twenty specific meta-intelligence tools and techniques you can use to help students learn about their intelligences. These tools and techniques are organized according to the four meta-intelligence levels I discussed earlier, namely, the tacit, aware, strategic, and reflective levels. Each intelligence lesson and its extensions include the functions of the intelligences, descriptions of personal strengths and weaknesses, ideas for what students can do to improve and strengthen all ways of knowing, and experiments in helping others utilize the full spectrum of their intellectual capabilities. Chapter 5 looks toward the future through a scenario of the "multiple intelligence school." The chapter explores implications of multiple intelligences for restructuring schools in four areas: curriculum, instruction, the learning process, and assessment. (For more information about each of these areas, see Lazear 1991a, 1991b, and 1994).

This book provides advanced help for teachers who are working with multiple intelligences in their classrooms, by both teaching students the skills of the intelligences and integrating multiple ways of knowing and learning in the daily teaching of various subjects. *Seven Pathways* assumes that you have been able to catalyze your students' interest in the seven ways of knowing. The tools and techniques presented in these pages are most effective when students are genuinely interested in learning more about themselves and "how they tick" intellectually. If that interest is not there already, or if it is weak, the tacit tools will likely be most useful as catalysts of the desire to learn more.

I believe that, with careful planning, you can easily integrate most of the tools and techniques I suggest into your daily lessons. Any time you can spend focusing on the intelligences as the content of the lesson, however, will not only increase students' awareness of the seven ways of knowing, but will also strengthen their abilities to use the intelligences skillfully in mastering assigned classroom material. The findings of all the research on metacognition indicate that the more aware students become about various learning processes in general and their own unique learning in particular, the better learners they will be, not only in school, but in their lives beyond the classroom as well.

Here is what you will find in chapters 1 through 4:

- **Twenty meta-intelligence activity lessons.** These lessons are intended to be the content focus of a lesson, providing students with an opportunity to explore and learn about their own and each other's various ways of knowing (see p. 13). Some of these lessons extend over several days and, in at least one case, over several weeks. I do not mean to suggest that you must spend an inordinate amount of time doing the lessons. I do suggest, however, that when you are using meta-intelligence tools that take more time, you give students a few minutes each day to reflect on the intelligence explorations and discoveries that they are making. This reflection is important because if students are experiencing difficulty with certain aspects of a given lesson or tool, you and other students can assist them, and the very act of students' sharing what is happening to them may serve to heighten and intensify their work with the lesson. The most important part of each lesson is the reflection at the end, so make sure you allow plenty of time for it.

- **One hundred twenty academic lesson extensions.** These extensions, which follow each lesson, are designed to help you teach about multiple intelligences in and through daily classroom academic material and thus are easily integrated into content-based lessons.

- **A set of reproducible materials for elementary, middle, and high school levels for each lesson.** You can use these materials to help you introduce an activity to your students. You will need to adapt the lesson procedures so they are appropriate to whatever grade level you teach. Remember Jerome Bruner's important insight about the "spiral curriculum": anything can be taught to any age level, if the teacher takes the time to step inside students' worldviews and speak the language those students can understand. I have provided spiraled reproducibles to help you step inside your students' worldviews. I am asking you to create the necessary spiraled lesson procedures from the meta-intelligence activity lessons.

- **A teacher's personal reflection log after each activity lesson.**
As I mentioned earlier, the metacognitive reflection time with students at the end of each lesson is important, so I believe you will find that these logs are vital. They provide you with an opportunity to move your own teaching for, with, and about multiple intelligences through the four meta-intelligence levels.
- **Notes for parents at the end of each chapter.** I have included these pages on the assumption that parents are a critical part of teaching students about multiple intelligences. Parents must understand what you are doing and why, especially given that this way of teaching and learning is quite different from the traditional educational system in the West. However, even if you do not have a high level of parental involvement, you can still teach your students about their intelligences very effectively.

These notes could be the basis for special in-service training sessions that teach parents how to help their children be more successful in school. You could use the notes to inform parents about multiple intelligence learning and teaching in parent-teacher conferences. Or you could simply give the notes to parents as information to help them understand what you are doing in the classroom and to assure them that it is based on solid educational research.

I also feel it is very important for teachers to share with their principal, other administrative personnel, and fellow teachers what they are doing in the classroom. The notes for parents at the end of this introduction give a helpful overview of the theory and practice of multiple intelligences. These pages may give administrators and colleagues basic background information. If they want more, I suggest they read *Seven Ways of Knowing* (Lazear 1991a), which contains a thorough introduction and comprehensive explanation of each intelligence.

You might also invite interested colleagues to observe lessons that apply multiple intelligences to the teaching and learning process. Ask your colleagues to interview students about the students' views on a multiple intelligences approach to teaching and learning. And even ask the observers to look at test scores and other appropriate multiple intelligence academic assessment methods that you are using in your classroom. My guess is that you will be able to show observers that many students who never have succeeded before are succeeding in school. And, of course, the observers will see highly motivated, active learning taking place!

Kitbag of Methods, Tools, and Techniques
for Teaching about Multiple Intelligences

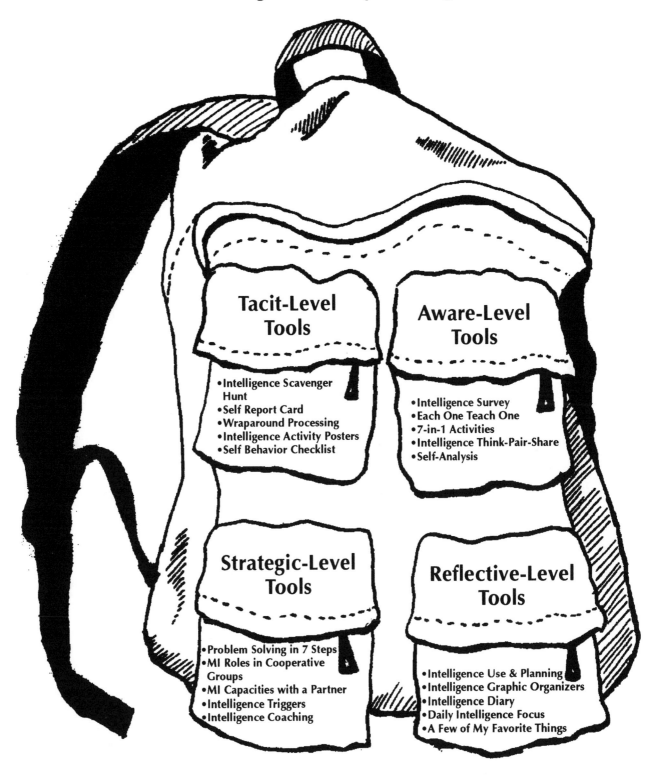

Tacit-Level Tools

- Intelligence Scavenger Hunt
- Self Report Card
- Wraparound Processing
- Intelligence Activity Posters
- Self Behavior Checklist

Aware-Level Tools

- Intelligence Survey
- Each One Teach One
- 7-in-1 Activities
- Intelligence Think-Pair-Share
- Self-Analysis

Strategic-Level Tools

- Problem Solving in 7 Steps
- MI Roles in Cooperative Groups
- MI Capacities with a Partner
- Intelligence Triggers
- Intelligence Coaching

Reflective-Level Tools

- Intelligence Use & Planning
- Intelligence Graphic Organizers
- Intelligence Diary
- Daily Intelligence Focus
- A Few of My Favorite Things

NOTES TO PARENTS

An Overview of the Seven Intelligences*

Although some of the latest brain research has revealed that we have many ways of being intelligent, the standardized testing we do in our schools does not address the full range of intellectual abilities and skills that we all have. Following is a description of seven such "ways of knowing." This description is based on the research Dr. Howard Gardner conducted at Harvard University. I have also included a list of exercises to help you access these intelligences in yourself and your children.

* Permission to reprint this section was kindly granted by Phi Delta Kappa (from their Fastback series).

Verbal/Linguistic Intelligence

We use our verbal/linguistic intelligence when we speak to each other, whether through formal speech or informal conversation. We use this intelligence when we put our thoughts down on paper, create poetry, or simply write a letter to a friend. Verbal/linguistic intelligence is involved in storytelling and creating, in all forms of humor that involve such things as plays on words, in the unexpected ending in a joke, and in various funny twists of the language. This intelligence is involved in any use of metaphors, similes, and analogies, and, of course, in learning proper grammar and syntax in speaking and writing.

Exercises to Stimulate Verbal/Linguistic Intelligence

- Choose a word randomly from the dictionary and practice working it into normal conversations with other people.
- Get a book of word games and puzzles (for example, crosswords, jumbles, and so on) or play language-oriented table games (for example, Scrabble™, Spill and Spell™, and so on).
- Watch a TV drama or detective story, then write your own sequel, or tell what you think should happen in the next episode.
- Talk with someone about his or her ideas or opinions. Ask questions, have a discussion, or engage in friendly debate.
- Make a presentation on a topic that interests and excites you (for example, a hobby, a political view, a book you've read, or someone you know).

Logical/Mathematical Intelligence

You can see logical/mathematical intelligence in operation most clearly when you are involved in a situation that requires problem solving or meeting a new challenge. This intelligence is often associated with what we call "scientific thinking." We use our logical/mathematical intelligence when we recognize abstract patterns, such as counting by twos or knowing if we've received the right change at the supermarket. We use it when we find connections or see relationships between seemingly separate and distinct pieces of information. Logical/mathematical intelligence is responsible for the various patterns of thinking we use in our daily lives, such as making lists, setting priorities, and planning something for the future.

Exercises to Stimulate Logical/Mathematical Intelligence

- Practice analytical thinking by classifying a group of twelve randomly gathered objects. See if you can create a rationale for organizing them (for example, shape, color, size, use, and so on).
- Do a project that requires following step-by-step directions, for example, building something that is not prefab or cooking from scratch.
- Create a four-point outline telling about a movie you have seen; each of the points will have four subpoints, and each subpoint will have four more subpoints.
- Create a convincing, rational argument for something that is ridiculous, such as why a family pet should be allowed to sit at the table and eat with the family.
- Create a sequence of numbers that have a hidden pattern. See if someone else can discover the pattern.

Visual/Spatial Intelligence

Visual/spatial intelligence can be seen in its purest form in the active imagination of children involved in such things as daydreaming, pretending to make themselves invisible, or imagining themselves to be on a great journey to magical times and places. We employ this intelligence when we draw pictures to express our thoughts and feelings, or when we decorate a room to create a certain mood. We use it when we use a map successfully to get someplace we want to go. Visual/spatial intelligence helps us win at chess, enables us to turn a blueprint on paper into a "real" object (for example, a bookshelf or a dress), and allows us to visualize things we want in our lives (for example, new curtains or wallpaper, a successful speech, a trip, a career change, or an award).

Exercises to Stimulate Visual/Spatial Intelligence

- Look at the clouds with a group of friends and see if you can find such things as animals, people, objects, faces, and so on, hidden in the formations.
- Practice exercises for using the active imagination; for example, imagine yourself living in a different period of history or pretend you are having a conversation with your hero, a character from literature, or a historical figure.
- Try to express an idea, opinion, or feeling with clay, paints, colored markers, or pens. Use images, shapes, patterns, designs, textures, and colors.

- Plan a scavenger hunt with friends. Make complex and interesting maps for each other to follow that will lead to the "treasure."
- Create a picture montage based on a theme or idea that interests you. Cut out a number of pictures from magazines and arrange them to convey what you want to say.

Bodily/Kinesthetic Intelligence

Bodily/kinesthetic intelligence would be seen in operation if I gave you a typewriter, with no markings on the keys, and asked you to type a letter. If at some time in your life you learned how to type, your fingers would "know" the keyboard and would likely be able to produce the letter with little or no effort at all. The body knows many things that are not necessarily known by the conscious mind, for example, how to ride a bike, park a car, catch an object, or maintain balance while walking. Bodily/kinesthetic intelligence also involves the ability to use the body to express emotions and thoughts (such as in dance or body language), to play an athletic or sporting game, to invent a new product, and to convey ideas (such as charades, mime, and drama).

Exercises to Stimulate Bodily/Kinesthetic Intelligence

- After a presentation, have everyone in a group express her or his reactions to the presentation through a physical gesture, action, movement, posture, or other body language.
- Pay attention to your body when you are involved in everyday, physical tasks such as shoveling snow, washing dishes, or fixing your car. See if you can become aware of what your body "knows" how to do and how it functions.
- Perform different physical activities, such as walking, dancing, or jogging. Try to match your mood. Also try some activities to change your mood.
- Practice using your nondominant hand to perform any taken-for-granted task, for example, brushing your teeth, eating, buttoning a shirt, and so on. See if you can train the hand to function more effectively.
- Try role-playing to express an idea, opinion, or feeling, or play "Modern-Day Inventions Charades."

Musical/Rhythmic Intelligence

We use our musical/rhythmic intelligence when we play music to calm or to stimulate ourselves. Many of us use music and rhythm to maintain a steady rhythm when jogging, cleaning the house, or learning to type. Musical/rhythmic intelligence is involved when you hear a jingle on the radio and find yourself humming it over and over throughout the day. This intelligence is active when we use tones and rhythmic patterns (instrumental, environmental, and human) to communicate how we are feeling and what we believe (for example the sounds of intense joy, fear, excitement, and loss), or to express the depth of our religious devotion or the intensity of our national loyalty.

Exercises to Stimulate Musical/Rhythmic Intelligence

- Make a list of different types of music you own or have access to. Listen to several minutes of each type and note how each affects you, for example, feelings and images it evokes, memories it sparks, and so on.
- Think of something you want to remember or something you want to teach someone. Choose a well-known tune and create a simple song using the information you want to remember or teach.
- Experiment expressing your feelings (for example, fear, contentment, anger, exhaustion, exhilaration, and so on) through vocal sounds only (no words!). Try producing different volumes, pitches, tones, and noises to communicate your meaning.
- Listen to the natural rhythmic patterns of your environment, for example, coffee brewing, traffic, the wind blowing, rain beating on the window, and so on. See what you can learn from these rhythms and beats.
- Read a story and practice "illustrating" it with various sound effects, music, rhythmic beats, tones—much like the old-time radio shows.

Interpersonal Intelligence

We experience our interpersonal intelligence most directly whenever we are part of a team effort, whether it be a sports team, a church committee, or a community task force. This intelligence utilizes our ability to engage in verbal and nonverbal communication and our capacity to notice distinctions among ourselves, for example, contrasts in moods, temperament, motivations, and intentions. Interpersonal intelligence allows us to develop a genuine sense of empathy and caring for each other. Through our interpersonal intelligence we can "stand in another's

Seven Pathways of Learning © 1994 Zephyr Press, Tucson, Arizona

shoes" and understand another person's feelings, fears, anticipations, and beliefs. This person-to-person way of knowing is the one through which we maintain our individual identity, but we also become "more than ourselves" as we identify with and become a part of others.

Exercises to Stimulate Interpersonal Intelligence

- Get a partner to try to reproduce a complex shape or design you have drawn. These are the rules: (1) Give verbal instructions only. (2) Your partner may not look at the drawing. (3) Your partner may ask you any question. (4) You may not look at what your partner is drawing.
- Explore different ways to express encouragement and support for other people (for example, facial expressions, body posture, gestures, sounds, words, and phrases). Practice giving encouragement and support to others around you each day.
- Practice listening deeply to someone who is expressing a view with which you disagree. Cut off the tendency to interpret what the person is saying and to express your own views. Force yourself to stay focused on what the person is saying. Try to paraphrase his or her thoughts to verify your own understanding.
- Volunteer to be part of a team and watch for positive and negative team behavior (positive team behavior includes the things that help the team work together and be successful; negative behavior includes the things that impair the team's efforts).
- Try disciplined people-watching, guessing what others are thinking and feeling, their backgrounds, professions, and so on, based on nonverbal clues (for example, dress, gestures, voice tone, colors, and so on). When possible (and appropriate!), check your accuracy with the person.

Intrapersonal Intelligence

Intrapersonal intelligence is the introspective intelligence. Intrapersonal intelligence allows us to be self-reflective, that is, to step back from ourselves and watch ourselves, almost like an outside observer. As far as we know, we are the only creatures gifted with such an ability. Intrapersonal intelligence involves a knowledge about and an awareness of the internal aspects of the self such as feelings, thinking processes, self-reflection, and intuition about spiritual realities. Both self-identity and the ability to transcend the self are part of the functioning of intrapersonal intelligence. When we experience a sense of unity, have an intuition about our connection with the larger order of things, experience higher states of consciousness, feel the lure of the future, and dream of unrealized potentials in our lives, it is the result of our intrapersonal way of knowing.

Exercises to Stimulate Intrapersonal Intelligence

- Make a mood graph that shows the high points and low points (as well as points in between) of your day. Note the external events that contributed to your different moods.
- Evaluate the thinking strategies and thinking patterns you use in different situations (for example, a problem arises in a well-planned activity, an emergency occurs, or you have to decide among a number of viable and attractive options).
- When doing something boring, try to be aware of all aspects of the activity: your movements, feelings, thoughts, the taste in your mouth, the smell in the air, the textures, the sounds, and so on.
- Create an experimental reflection log in which you record key events from your day. Then, using such things as paints, music, clay, and poetry, express your feelings about those events.
- Pretend you are an outside observer watching your thoughts, feelings, and moods. Notice different patterns that seem to arise in certain situations, for example, the "anger pattern," the "playfulness pattern," or the "anxiety pattern."

The following diagram includes a summary of the capacities and skills related to each of the intelligences. These skills must be taught explicitly to students if the students are to learn how to use all seven ways of knowing. Just as students must be taught the alphabet, how to make words, and how to read and write if they are to be strong in verbal/linguistic intelligence, they must be taught such things as how to use the active imagination, how to do graphic representation, and how to see relationships between different objects in space if they are to be strong in visual/spatial intelligence. I suggest that you use this wheel as a checklist to evaluate your children's relative strengths and weaknesses in each intelligence area. Then use some of the activities suggested at the end of the chapters in this book to give your children opportunities to exercise and practice using all of their intelligences at home.

Multiple Intelligence Capacities Inventory Wheel*

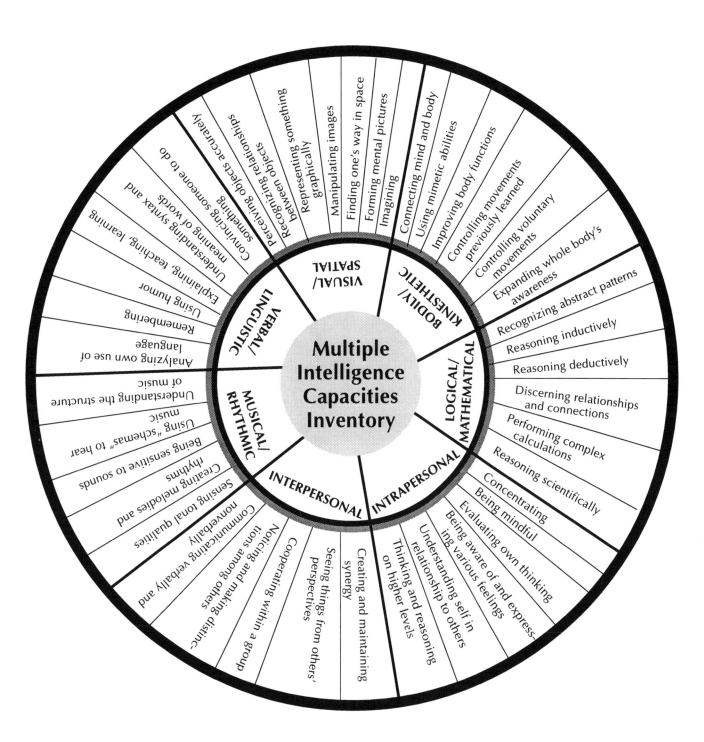

* Adapted from David Lazear's *Seven Ways of Knowing: Understanding Multiple Intelligences,* 2nd ed. (Palatine, Ill.: Skylight Publishing, 1991).

=1=
Activities for Tacit
Use of the Intelligences

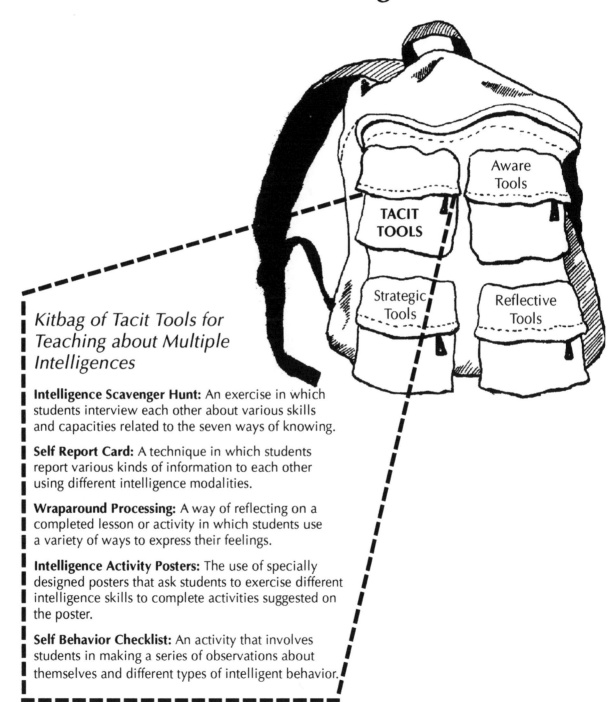

Kitbag of Tacit Tools for Teaching about Multiple Intelligences

Intelligence Scavenger Hunt: An exercise in which students interview each other about various skills and capacities related to the seven ways of knowing.

Self Report Card: A technique in which students report various kinds of information to each other using different intelligence modalities.

Wraparound Processing: A way of reflecting on a completed lesson or activity in which students use a variety of ways to express their feelings.

Intelligence Activity Posters: The use of specially designed posters that ask students to exercise different intelligence skills to complete activities suggested on the poster.

Self Behavior Checklist: An activity that involves students in making a series of observations about themselves and different types of intelligent behavior.

Billy was a third-grade student who was not doing very well in school. He had some strange ideas and some strange ways of behaving in the classroom. He rarely succeeded at assigned classroom work, on tests, or on his homework. He did not have many friends because the other children thought that he was dumb and some kind of a "weirdo."

Billy's teacher had received training in working with the seven intelligences in the classroom. She decided to share these seven ways of knowing with the class by having the students work in small groups on an Intelligence Activities poster (see pp. 42–48). Suddenly Billy came alive; he was able to do some of the things on the poster that others in his group could not. The teacher told the class that all of the ideas on the poster are the different ways we are smart. Billy's hand shot up immediately.

He said, "These are things that I do every day. I usually feel like I'm kind of dumb. But I was really good at some of the things on the poster! I never thought of these things as making me smart in a different way!"

The teacher asked Billy's team to share some of their thoughts about and experiences of working on the poster. Some of the comments follow:

> *We would have failed if Billy hadn't been in our group. He could do some of the things none of the rest of us could!*

> *Everyone in the group could do something, but no one could do everything.*

> *I could sort of do everything on the poster, but some people were really good!*

> *I'm glad I didn't have to do it alone!*

Other groups shared similar reflections.

Needless to say, this simple activity had a dramatic impact on the class. Suddenly their perception of what makes someone smart had changed. And, what is more important, their perception of Billy and Billy's perception of himself had changed.

Seven Pathways of Learning © 1994 Zephyr Press, Tucson, Arizona

INTELLIGENCE SCAVENGER HUNT

Lesson Procedures

1. Create eight interview questions that students will use to ask each other about the seven intelligences (see examples on the work sheet on pp. 28–30).
2. Have each student secretly decide which two activities on the Scavenger Hunt work sheet he or she performs best.
3. Give your students the following instructions before the Scavenger Hunt actually begins:

> *Get up out of your seats. Each of you will find eight different people who can each do the activity in one of the boxes. When you find someone who can do the activity, have that person sign your work sheet. You need only one name per box, but you cannot repeat a name; you are to get eight different names.*
>
> *When you are talking with the other students, do not take their word that they can do the activities listed in the boxes. Make them prove it to you by performing! Once each person has demonstrated the skill, have him or her sign your work sheet in the appropriate box.*
>
> *Watch yourself and watch each other as you are involved in the activity. See what you can learn about yourself and about each other.*

4. Ask the class if they have any questions about the assignment. If not, then tell them to begin going about the classroom, looking for students who meet the criteria on the work sheets. Give students ten to fifteen minutes to do the activity, depending on how you sense things are going as you walk around.
5. While the students are doing the Scavenger Hunt, watch them carefully and make notes about what you observe. You may want to share some of these observations with them later.

Intelligence Scavenger Hunt

INTRODUCTION

This activity is a great strategy for helping students learn about the seven intelligences from others' experience. Students interview each other, looking for different skills and capacities in fellow classmates. Some students have called it a "human treasure hunt."

OBJECTIVE

The purposes of this lesson are to help students become aware of, appreciate, and enjoy the differences that exist among them and to become aware of their own skills and capacities, including their strengths and preferences in certain areas.

DISCUSSION

Further applications of the Scavenger Hunt strategy are limited only by your imagination. Remember that this is a learning process, and the key is to have students discover information and knowledge by asking each other questions. It is important that you have the whole class reflect on what they learned while they did their Scavenger Hunt. You may also want to collect their work sheets, especially if you are using the work sheets to help you assess students' comprehension of a lesson or unit or to evaluate their academic progress.

6. When the students have finished the activity, have them return to their seats and lead them in the following discussion:

- *Which activity was the easiest to find someone for?* (Ask who signed that box and what he or she said or did.)
- *Which activity was the hardest to find someone for?*
- *What did you find interesting? What surprised you? Excited you?*
- *What did you learn about yourself? What did you learn about each other?* (You might also share any observations you made.)
- *What are some of your ideas about how we could use the Scavenger Hunt again?*
- *How could we use some of the skills you discovered in the Scavenger Hunt in our classroom work?*

Intelligence Scavenger Hunt Extensions

More Intelligence Scavenger Hunt Ideas

The following are ideas you may adapt to your academic content.

- **Getting Acquainted.** Use an Intelligence Scavenger Hunt at the beginning of the year to help students get to know each other and to learn about their summers. Include questions that require students to use the seven ways of knowing as they look for others to sign their work sheets.

- **Review.** Create an Intelligence Scavenger Hunt in which students must find people who know the answers to various questions about a completed unit of study. Make sure that the work sheets include questions that use all seven intelligences.

- **Assessing Prior Knowledge.** At the beginning of a new unit of study, create an Intelligence Scavenger Hunt to find out what students already know about the content of the upcoming unit. Design questions that explore all the levels of the unit as well as students' feelings about and anticipation of it.

- **Intelligence Capacities Exploration.** Design an Intelligence Scavenger Hunt for *each* of the seven intelligences. The questions should allow students to explore the various capacities/skills of the seven ways of knowing (see the Capacities Inventory Wheel on p. 21). Make sure the questions are appropriate for the intelligence; for example, don't ask students to give verbal or written responses for an intelligence that is basically nonverbal!

- **Reinforcing Learning.** Design a process-oriented Intelligence Scavenger Hunt in which students not only explain various processes (for example, in math, science, P.E., industrial and home arts) to each other, but also demonstrate those processes.

- **New Learning.** Put students into different "expert groups" that are responsible for mastering new concepts, processes, definitions, and so on. Each group must learn its assigned piece and then teach it to others during the Intelligence Scavenger Hunt activity. Base the Intelligence Scavenger Hunt on the expert groups and the concepts they were assigned.

- **Homework Processing.** Use an Intelligence Scavenger Hunt to have students discuss the previous night's homework, correct it, and check for understanding. Create questions that are related to the specific elements of the homework assignment. Students must find other students who know the answers.

- **Post-Test Relearning.** At the conclusion of an examination, create an Intelligence Scavenger Hunt with wrong answers from the test. Students must find others who can explain why the answer is wrong and demonstrate how to get the right answer. After this activity, let students take the test again.

Intelligence Scavenger Hunt
(Elementary)

Find someone who . . .

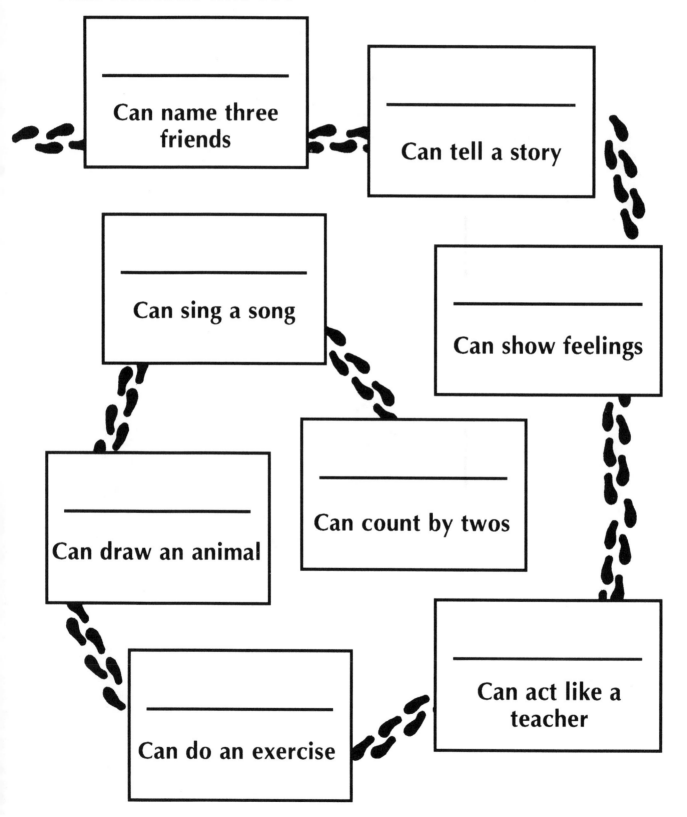

_____

Can name three friends

_____

Can tell a story

_____

Can sing a song

_____

Can show feelings

_____

Can draw an animal

_____

Can count by twos

_____

Can do an exercise

_____

Can act like a teacher

Intelligence Scavenger Hunt
(Middle School)

Find someone who . . .

Can list three things that help her or him learn.

Can draw a picture of his or her favorite food.

Can tell what it's like to be on a team.

Has a physical game she or he likes to play.

Has something he or she likes to do by him- or herself.

Likes to read or write or has a good joke to tell.

Will sing part of a favorite song.

Likes to solve puzzles or is good at math.

Intelligence Scavenger Hunt
(Secondary)

Find someone who . . .

_____

Sings in the shower
and with the radio
when riding in a car.

_____

Can solve a variety of math
problems (including getting
the correct change).

_____

Has some special thing
she or he does to relax
and renew her- or himself.

_____

Can name three things
necessary for effective
teamwork.

_____

Can draw a picture
about what kind of day
he or she is having.

_____

Can list at least five different
ways people learn, know,
and understand.

_____

Loves to dance or is involved
in some type of daily
physical exercise.

_____

Loves to read and write
and is good at expressing
him- or herself in words.

Teacher's Personal Reflection Log

INTELLIGENCE SCAVENGER HUNT

I have the following thoughts/insights about the Intelligence Scavenger Hunt strategy:

I feel that the Intelligence Scavenger Hunt strategy can help me in my teaching in the following ways:

As a learning process, the Intelligence Scavenger Hunt strategy includes the following benefits for my students:

I have the following specific ideas for using the Intelligence Scavenger Hunt strategy in my classroom in the near future:

I think the Intelligence Scavenger Hunt strategy can be used beyond the classroom and school in the following ways:

Self Report Card

INTRODUCTION

The Self Report Card is a wonderful activity for making students aware of their own intelligence "comfort zones." The process asks students to share things about themselves in the different intelligence areas that the students like.

OBJECTIVE

The goal of this lesson is to make students aware that they have all seven ways of knowing, but that they are more comfortable with and probably better at some than at others.

DISCUSSION

The Self Report Card strategy asks students to be slightly introspective because they have to be aware of which intelligences they prefer. Initially, however, they will not know that the things about which you are asking them to report are intelligences. They become aware on the tacit level when you reflect on the lesson, helping them to see and appreciate the fact that we are different. The gimmick of having them exchange report cards with each other and asking about things on the card makes them more willing to risk, since the card appears to be the point of dialogue, not the person.

SELF REPORT CARD

Lesson Procedures

1. Pass out a large index card and some colored marking pens to each student.
2. Tell the students that they are each going to create a report card to evaluate themselves and some of the things they can and like to do. Choose six areas, such as those on the model report card on the work sheet (see p. 35). Project the questions on an overhead or write them on the board.
3. Give students several minutes to record their answers to the questions in the six spaces on their index cards.
4. Explain the task to the class:

   > *In a moment I am going to ask you to get out of your seats and start sharing your report cards with each other. Find one other person with whom to exchange report cards. Choose one or two things that especially interest you from your partner's report card and ask her or him to tell you about it and do it for you. For example, if someone says she can make a funny face, have her do it. If someone says he can sing a song, have him sing it.*
   >
   > *After each of you has had a chance to share at least two things on your report card, get your own card back and move to someone else. Your goal is to see how many people you can talk with in ten to fifteen minutes. Watch yourself and each other and see what you can learn about these different skills.*

5. Ask if there are any questions. If not, tell the students to begin. Watch them carefully so that you can give feedback during the discussion time.
6. After the allotted time has elapsed, call the class back together and lead them in the following discussion:

- *Without mentioning any names, what was the most interesting thing you found someone else could do?*
- *What did you find out that was surprising? That was not surprising?*
- *What were your feelings about doing the Self Report Card activity? What did you like? What did you not like?*
- *What did you learn about yourself? About each other?*

On the board or overhead list ideas about how to use these different capacities in schoolwork.

Self Report Card Extensions

More Self Report Card Ideas

The following are ideas you may adapt to your academic content.

- **Key "Learnings" Report.** At the conclusion of a unit of study create a Self Report Card that asks students to share different things from the unit or lesson that have been significant for them: most important idea, a surprise, a new question raised, a point of confusion, and so on.

- **Applications Report.** As a way to help students with the transfer or "bridging" of learning beyond the classroom, design a Self Report Card on potential applications of a lesson or unit: Where in the past have students applied the skill? What places can students think of to use it today? What possible applications does the skill have for the future?

- **Affective Report.** In the various corners of the Self Report Card have each student write a word or phrase, draw a symbol or picture, make a sound or sing a song, and do a physical gesture or make a body movement that expresses a feeling about something you are studying.

- **Connections Report.** Ask students to think of another subject they are studying in school as it relates to the current subject. On their Report Cards have them list one cross-discipline connection they see between the current lesson or unit and things they are learning in other classes or subjects. They should try to think of one such connection per corner of the card.

- **Report Card "Jeopardy."** For each corner of their Report Cards, give students an answer to a question that could be on a test about the unit or lesson you are studying. Students are to write a question for the answer you have given, then share their questions by exchanging report cards.

- **Specific Intelligence Focus "Reports."** Create a Self Report Card based on the capacities/skills of each intelligence, for example, a visual/spatial report card, an intrapersonal report card, and so on. Make sure that the categories you create for the different corners of the card imply the necessity of demonstrating particular capacities and skills (see the Capacities Inventory Wheel on p. 21).

Seven Pathways of Learning © 1994 Zephyr Press, Tucson, Arizona

Self Report Card
(All Grades)

Write a big word.	Draw your house.	Sing a song or say a rhyme.

Name _____

How high can you count?	Do something funny.	"I'm happy when . . . "

Name something you read recently (outside of schoolwork).	Write down a favorite song that you are able to sing.	List three words that express your feelings about math.

Name _____

Write down a physical exercise that you are able and willing to do.	Draw your bedroom as it looks now.	Finish the sentence: "When I'm alone I like to . . . "

Name something you read recently that was important to you.	Draw a symbol to show your feelings about today.	Write down a favorite song or type of music. (You must be able to perform it.)

Name _____

On a scale of 1 to 10, rank your math problem-solving ability.	Write down a physical feat you can and would perform.	What do you do for personal renewal?

Teacher's Personal Reflection Log

SELF REPORT CARD

I have the following thoughts/insights about the Self Report Card strategy:

I feel that the Self Report Card strategy can help me in my teaching in the following ways:

As a learning process, the Self Report Card strategy includes the following benefits for my students:

I have the following specific ideas for using the Self Report Card strategy in my classroom in the near future:

I think the Self Report Card strategy can be used beyond the classroom and school in the following ways:

Seven Pathways of Learning © 1994 Zephyr Press, Tucson, Arizona

WRAPAROUND PROCESSING

Lesson Procedures

1. At the conclusion of a lesson or activity, give students time to think about their individual responses to the lesson or activity using the seven intelligences (see "stem" examples on the work sheet, p. 40).

2. After students have had time to do their own thinking, have them each turn to a partner and share their seven responses to the lesson or activity. They are not only to talk about their responses; they are to show each other images, do gestures, make sounds, sing a few bars of their songs, and share their ideas about the importance of the lesson for our times and themselves. Tell the students to pay close attention to the various ways in which their partners respond, for they will be asked to reproduce what their partners do for other partners later.

3. Now have each student turn to a different partner and share by doing the *previous* partner's responses to the lesson or activity.

4. After the class has had time to share in this manner, call them back together. Lead them in the following discussion, making a list of the responses on the overhead or board:

   - *What are some of the words you heard others say that expressed their feelings about the lesson or activity?*
   - *What kind of thinking did this lesson cause us to use?*
   - *Have several students come to the board and draw images that express some of the feelings about the lesson or activity. The images should be ones they learned from one of their partners. Ask the students, "What common patterns or designs do you see as you look at all of the images?"*
   - *On the count of three, everyone makes a gesture that expresses feelings about the lesson or activity. The gestures should be ones they learned from a partner.*

Wraparound Processing

INTRODUCTION

You can use the Wraparound Processing technique (also known as a "stem") at the end of any lesson or activity to help students reflect on and share their feelings about the lesson or activity. This activity is a great "instant thermometer" that reveals how the students feel about and what they have learned from the lesson or activity.

OBJECTIVE

The goal of this lesson is to help students realize that there are many ways to reflect on and process their feelings and thoughts about a classroom lesson or activity.

DISCUSSION

In some ways, the processing of a lesson is the most important part; during the processing, the knowing of the lesson is cemented in the brain/mind/body system. The keys to successful wraparound processing are (1) having "stems" that students want to answer, (2) accepting every answer that is given (there are no wrong answers), and (3) going around the room with the expectation that everyone will have an answer, allowing (but not encouraging) students to pass if they choose. You can often learn more about the impact a lesson has on students through the wraparound processing technique than through any other method.

Have students look around the room and ask them, "What common things do you see?"

- *Choose ten students to stand. Have each of the ten take turns making the sound or singing the song one of their partners would play as a background for the lesson or activity. Then, as if you were a conductor, randomly point to the different students and create a symphony of the background "music." Ask the class, "What does this sound or music tell us about the lesson?"*
- *Have several students relate ideas they heard from one of their partners about the importance of the lesson for people living in our times.*
- *Give students a few minutes to rewrite their statements about how they can use the information from this lesson or activity beyond the classroom (number 7 on the work sheet), incorporating ideas they got from their partners. Ask for several volunteers to share what they have written.*

5. Ask students, "How has this way of reflecting on a lesson or activity helped you appreciate the lesson? What other ideas do you have for using the seven ways of knowing to reflect on and discuss our lessons?"

Wraparound Processing Extensions

More Wraparound Processing Ideas

The following are ideas you may adapt to your academic content.

- **Capacities Wraparound.** Design your Wraparound Processing stems around the specific capacities of an intelligence (refer to wheel on p. 21). If you have been emphasizing musical or rhythmic intelligence, for example, you might have your students beat out a rhythm, make vocal sounds, hum a popular tune, write a simple song, imagine different environmental sounds, and so on.

- **Wraparound by Groups.** At the end of a lesson have students huddle quickly with three or four people near them. Together they will discuss their individual responses using the wraparound processing stems. For each stem, the groups are to reach a consensus on the response that represents most accurately the feelings of the team. All team members must agree and be able to explain the team's response.

- **Mural Wraparound.** Paper one wall of the room with newsprint and give each student a colored marker. At the end of the lesson have all students go to the newsprint and create a mural about the lesson. Have students talk with those on either side of them so that their contributions to the mural blend with what others are doing.

- **Tableaux Wraparound.** At the conclusion of a lesson or unit quickly place students in groups of five. They are to turn themselves into a "human sculpture" that expresses the main ideas and points of the lesson or unit. Each group presents itself to the rest of the class, which tries to guess the meaning of the sculpture.

- **Sound Wraparound.** Have each student think of a sound that represents or expresses the lesson just completed. Count to three and have students make their sounds, then have them find and stand by others who are making a similar sound. Pretend that the class is an orchestra. Point to different groups and have them make their sounds on a cue from you. Afterward, have students reflect on what these sounds tell us about the lesson.

- **Piggyback Wraparound.** Have each student create a three-to-five-word phrase about his or her experience of the lesson. Have one volunteer share the phrase. The next student must piggyback a phrase on what the previous student said. One student might say, for example, "The lesson was difficult and demanding." The second student might respond, "Yes, the lesson was difficult and demanding, and this struggle caused me to think about some new things." A third student might add, "Yes, the lesson caused me to think about some new things, and it also made me have some new questions."

Wraparound Processing
(All Grades)

Elementary: Do each part with the whole class; have individuals make suggestions that the class performs.

Middle: Have students work through the steps with a team and share with the whole class.

Secondary: Have students work through the steps individually, then share with a partner or with the whole class.

1. **Write three words about the lesson.**

2. **What kind of thinking did the lesson cause you to do?**

3. **Draw an image or picture about the lesson.**

4. **Make up a body movement or gesture about the lesson.**

5. **What sound or song would you play as background to the lesson?**

6. **Discuss with a partner how the information from the lesson is important and can be applied today.**

7. **Finish the sentence: "This lesson is important to me because . . . "**

Teacher's Personal Reflection Log
WRAPAROUND PROCESSING

I have the following thoughts/insights about the Wraparound Processing strategy:

I feel that the Wraparound Processing strategy can help me in my teaching in the following ways:

As a learning process, the Wraparound Processing strategy includes the following benefits for my students:

I have the following specific ideas for using the Wraparound Processing strategy in my classroom in the near future:

I think the Wraparound Processing strategy can be used beyond the classroom and school in the following ways:

Intelligence Activity Posters

INTRODUCTION

This activity engages students in a group exploration of their various intelligence skills or capacities. The posters provide a variety of fun and engaging activities. To complete the posters, students must help and learn from each other.

OBJECTIVE

The goal of the lesson is to reveal the importance of honoring and utilizing the unique gifts and skills of each member of a group.

DISCUSSION

Although this lesson relies heavily on visual/spatial intelligence, it can move students very effectively into a tacit awareness of the other intelligences as well. Obviously, the posters do not have to be as well developed or as sophisticated as the ones in the examples. The posters could even be made into activity sheets. Remember, however, the more intriguing and fun you can make the posters, the more you will hook students on doing the activity, and the greater the discoveries they will make.

INTELLIGENCE ACTIVITY POSTERS

Lesson Procedures

1. Divide students into groups of four and give each group a copy of a poster from the work sheets (see pp. 45–47).
2. Give the groups the following assignment:

   Look at the poster together and make sure you understand the various tasks or activities it is asking you to perform. You may ask me questions about anything you do not understand.

   Before beginning work on the poster, plan your strategy for completing the poster. Write down your plan and why you chose each part of the plan. Remember that there are no "right" reasons for your decisions. The only "right" is knowing the "why" for each step you decide to take.

   You have fifteen to twenty minutes to work on the poster and execute your plan.

   Observe the groups carefully as they work, making sure that you are available to answer questions and to help them through any difficulties.
3. After the students have completed their work, have each group join with another group to share what they have done. Make sure that they don't just talk about their work, but have them lead the other group in an *experiential report* of their work; that is, have them try to learn the tongue twister, try to guess the number pattern, try the exercise routine, and so on.
4. After the groups have completed their sharing, bring the class back together. Lead them in the following discussion:

   • *What are some of the things that happened as you were working on the poster with your group?*

Seven Pathways of Learning © 1994 Zephyr Press, Tucson, Arizona

- *What are some of the things that happened when you shared your work with another group?*
- *What are some of the feelings you experienced as you worked with your group? What was easy? What was hard?*
- *What surprised you? What was fun? Exciting? Frustrating?*
- *What did you learn about each other as you worked on the poster? What did you learn about yourself?*
- *What did we learn in this activity that will help us in our daily classroom work? What did you learn that will help you with your homework?*

Intelligence Activity Posters Extensions

More Intelligence Activity Poster Lesson Ideas

The following are ideas you may adapt to your academic content.

- **Application Posters.** Create an activity poster that asks students to apply certain things from a lesson or unit to everyday life situations (for example, dividing a cake into equal pieces to serve all people at the table, writing an argument to persuade parents to let one use the car on the weekend, and so on). Try to cover all the intelligences in the activities you design.

- **Curriculum Integration Posters.** In the center of the poster write a key concept or idea from a lesson that you know reverberates across the curriculum. Through the poster activities, have students make connections to other subjects or content areas. Make sure that you cover all curriculum areas: history, science, math, language arts, health, social studies, the fine arts, practical arts (home economics and shop), and P.E.

- **Concept Extension Posters.** Focus on a key concept from a lesson or unit you are studying. Create a poster that asks students to explore the concept using the seven ways of knowing; they may write about it, draw it, make up a song about it, act it out, analyze it, discuss it with others, meditate on it, and so on.

- **"Stump the Class" Posters.** Divide students into groups of three to four and have them create an activity poster of their own based on concepts from a completed lesson or unit. Have each group draw a concept from a hat and create an activity poster based on it. Each team presents its poster and the class tries to guess the concept behind the poster.

- **Future Lesson Input Posters.** Present a content outline of an upcoming unit of the curriculum. Have students get into small groups and create posters that suggest activities they would enjoy and that cover the assigned content. Collect the posters and use them to help you plan lessons for the unit.

- **One Poster per Intelligence.** Have students use the various capacities of the seven intelligences (see the Capacities Inventory Wheel on p. 21) to create an activity poster that is based on exploring and trying out each of these capacities. Make sure the various activities you ask students to do are intelligence appropriate, that is, they take students beyond mere discussion of the capacities.

Seven Pathways of Learning © 1994 Zephyr Press, Tucson, Arizona

Multiple Intelligence Activity Poster

(Elementary)

Can you count to 10?

1 _ _ _ _ _ _ _ _ 10

Can you add to 10?

1+2+3+4+5+6+7+8+9+10=

A B C D E

Can you make all the letters in the alphabet with your body? Try it!

I like to sit alone and think about . . .

7

Ways of Knowing

What makes a good friend?

1.
2.
3.

Make up a song about your family.

Make a pattern with the colors you like most!

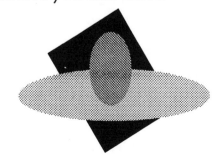

Tell a story about . . .

a pet
a party
an old person
water
a trip

Multiple Intelligence Activity Poster
(Middle School)

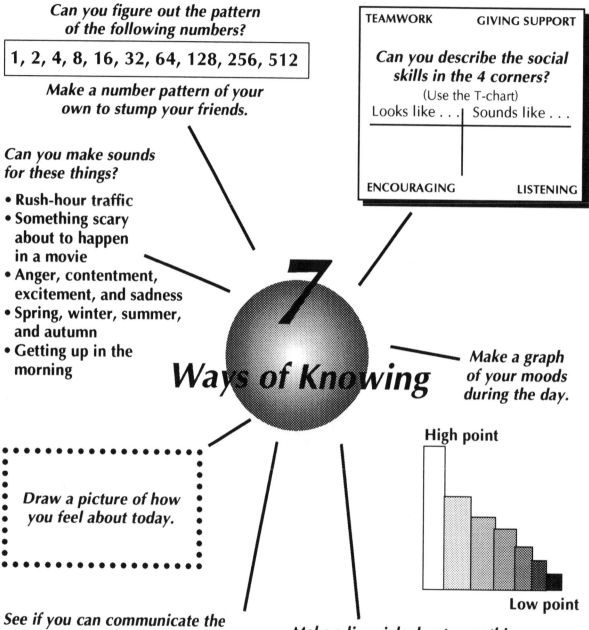

Can you figure out the pattern of the following numbers?

| 1, 2, 4, 8, 16, 32, 64, 128, 256, 512 |

Make a number pattern of your own to stump your friends.

Can you make sounds for these things?

• Rush-hour traffic
• Something scary about to happen in a movie
• Anger, contentment, excitement, and sadness
• Spring, winter, summer, and autumn
• Getting up in the morning

TEAMWORK   GIVING SUPPORT

Can you describe the social skills in the 4 corners?
(Use the T-chart)
Looks like . . . | Sounds like . . .

ENCOURAGING   LISTENING

Ways of Knowing

Make a graph of your moods during the day.

High point

Low point

Draw a picture of how you feel about today.

See if you can communicate the following things using only facial expressions and gestures:

• TOTAL BOREDOM
• GREAT FEAR
• SURPRIZE
• EXTREME HAPPINESS
• EXTREME INTEREST
• SADDNESS OR SORROW

Make a limerick about something that happened today. Example:

A pretty young girl named Rae,

Was having a wonderful day,

Until she went into math

Where her test she got back.

Now she has no idea what to say.

Seven Pathways of Learning © 1994 Zephyr Press, Tucson, Arizona

Multiple Intelligence Activity Poster
(Secondary)

List 10 examples of "math in everyday life."

1.
2.
3.
4.
5.
6.
7.
8.
9.
10.

Rank the list from most to least important to you.

?

What's it all about? My big questions about life are . . .

Write an exciting, fun paragraph about something very mundane, such as the examples that follow:

- BRUSHING YOUR TEETH
- DOING THE LAUNDRY
- EATING A HAMBURGER
- WALKING THE DOG

Make it sound as if it is the most important thing that ever has and ever will happen in human history.

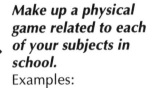

Make up a physical game related to each of your subjects in school.
Examples:

Science soccer
Math marathon
Social studies skating
Language arts archery

7 **Ways of Knowing**

Make the appropriate back-ground music or rhythm for the following:

- **Standing in the checkout line at the store**
- **Getting ready to go on a date, being on the date, after the date**
- **Doing the homework you get for each of your subjects**
- **Explaining a bad grade to your parents**
- **Being caught in rush-hour traffic**

What objects, persons, or animals can you find in this design?

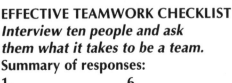

EFFECTIVE TEAMWORK CHECKLIST
Interview ten people and ask them what it takes to be a team.
Summary of responses:

1.   6.
2.   7.
3.   8.
4.   9.
5.   10.

Teacher's Personal Reflection Log
INTELLIGENCE ACTIVITY POSTERS

I have the following thoughts/insights about the Intelligence Activity Posters strategy:

I feel that the Intelligence Activity Posters strategy can help me in my teaching in the following ways:

As a learning process, the Intelligence Activity Posters strategy includes the following benefits for my students:

I have the following specific ideas for using the Intelligence Activity Posters strategy in my classroom in the near future:

I think the Intelligence Activity Posters strategy can be used beyond the classroom and school in the following ways:

Seven Pathways of Learning © 1994 Zephyr Press, Tucson, Arizona

SELF BEHAVIOR CHECKLIST

Lesson Procedures

1. Give each student a small notebook or have students create notebooks that will be their "intelligence tracking" logs for one week. The models on pages 52–54 give examples of how the logs could be set up.
2. Give students a few moments each day of the week to record things they have noticed about themselves under each of the categories of their logs.
3. At the end of the week, place students in groups of three. Have each group use the following criteria to create a three-way Venn diagram on a piece of newsprint that can be posted later. Have the students compare and contrast their logs with others using the Venn diagrams.

   1. things that were unique to each person
   2. things I had in common with one other person in the group
   3. things that we all had in common

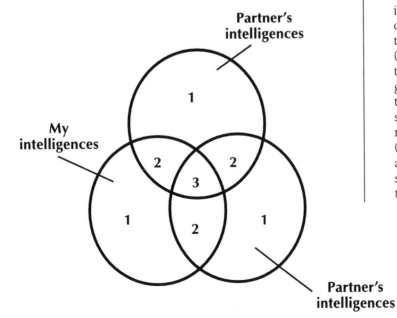

Self Behavior Checklist

INTRODUCTION

This activity asks students to track or pay attention to a number of their taken-for-granted behaviors and activities during the course of a normal week. As the week progresses students will find more and more skills they have rarely considered to be intellectually significant.

OBJECTIVE

The goal of the lesson is to help students recognize and name their "intelligent behavior" beyond the classroom and in activities that are not usually thought of as intelligence related.

DISCUSSION

Of all of the lessons in this chapter, the Self Behavior Checklist strategy requires the highest degree of introspection from your students. In some ways this activity requires students to be like detectives, seeking intelligence clues within taken-for-granted behavior patterns. Keys to the success of this strategy include (1) elevating it to the level of homework you expect students to complete during the week; (2) reminding students everyday to check their self behavior, maybe giving them a few minutes in class to work on their checklists (doing so will demonstrate your seriousness about the assignment); and (3) discussing how the checklists are coming, addressing difficulties students are experiencing in doing the assignment.

4. Have the groups post their Venns on the walls around the room. Have each group visit the other Venns and note the similarities and differences among their own Venns and those of the other groups.

5. Call the class back together for a discussion of what they have learned about their seven ways of being intelligent. On the overhead or board list the items they recorded on their Venns at the three-way intersections for each intelligence. Ask them the following questions:

   - *Is there anything that surprises you about this list?*
   - *What ideas do you have about how you could create an even greater awareness of how you use the seven intelligences in your daily life?*
   - *What could we do in this class to make ourselves more aware of the seven intelligences and how we use them everyday?*

6. Give students time to create a symbol that will remind them to be aware of the seven intelligences in their everyday lives. Ask the students to post their symbols on their walls at home and to draw the images in their notebooks in places where the students will see them often.

Self Behavior Checklist Extensions

More Self Behavior Checklist Lesson Ideas

The following are ideas you may adapt to your academic content.

- **Intelligence Capacities Checklists.** Create checklists that focus separately on the capacities or skills of each intelligence. Make sure the checklists are both developmentally and intelligence appropriate (see the Capacities Inventory Wheel on p. 21).

- **Past Experiences Checklist.** Have students create a checklist that illustrates the uses, experiences, and importance of particular concepts and ideas in a unit, things that the students may have used and experienced before. Have students talk with their parents and other adults, as well as examine their own lives from birth till the present, for examples.

- **Future Projection Checklist.** Have students create a checklist that illustrates potential future uses and experiences, and the importance of particular concepts and ideas you are teaching. Ask the students to think of ways a particular concept will or may be useful and necessary one hundred years from today. Then have students use their checklists to poll other people to see what those people think.

- **Other People Checklist.** Using the same basic behavior checklist as in the original lesson, assign students to watch for behavior that indicates the different intelligences in people the students know

outside of school, for example, their family, a church youth group, an after-school club, and so on. Have them track the occurrence of multiple intelligences in other people and report the findings to the class.

- **Lesson Reaction Checklist.** Create a checklist of possible reactions to a lesson, making sure that you include reactions for each intelligence. At the beginning of a lesson, hand out the checklist and ask students to watch themselves during the lesson, checking off anything on the list that is true of their experience of the lesson. Following are some examples:

    I was making pictures in my head to go along with the lesson.

    I wanted to get up out of my seat and do something.

    I wanted to talk with others about it.

- **Academic Subjects Checklist.** Have students make a list of the subjects they study in school. Have them create a checklist comprised of the capacities or skills of the different intelligences using the Capacities Inventory Wheel in the introduction. Ask students to carry the checklist with them for a week, looking for the intelligence capacities or skills that are part of the different subjects they are studying.

Self Behavior Checklist
(Elementary)

What did you do today?

- ☐ **Drew**

- ☐ **Counted**

- ☐ **Sang**

- ☐ **Wrote**

- ☐ **Talked**

- ☐ **Thought**

- ☐ **Played**

Self Behavior Checklist
(Middle School)

What did you do today?
Mark an "X" in the box beside each thing you did today.

- ☐ **Had an interesting conversation with someone**
- ☐ **Spent some time alone, thinking**
- ☐ **Listened to music**
- ☐ **Did some drawing**
- ☐ **Played a game that required me to use my body**
- ☐ **Used math to figure something out**
- ☐ **Did some singing (even in the shower!)**
- ☐ **Wrote something outside of assigned schoolwork**
- ☐ **Made something with my hands**
- ☐ **Got some exercise**
- ☐ **Spent some time just relaxing**
- ☐ **Watched a television show or a movie**
- ☐ **Expressed my feelings**
- ☐ **Read something interesting outside of my schoolwork**
- ☐ **Learned something new about another person**

Self Behavior Checklist
(Secondary)

What did you do today?

Look back on your day and put an "X" in the box
beside each behavior or activity that you did.

☐ I doodled during a lesson.

☐ I learned something new about myself.

☐ I had a great conversation with someone.

☐ I had an enjoyable experience listening to music.

☐ I used "applied math."

☐ I wrote something that pleases me.

☐ I got some physical exercise.

☐ I expressed myself using gestures and other body language.

☐ I was aware of colors.

☐ I read something outside of schoolwork that was interesting.

☐ I saw a pattern or design that I found interesting.

☐ I caught myself singing or humming a tune.

☐ I was aware of my feelings about something.

☐ I resolved a disagreement with another person.

☐ I learned something from a picture or a visual aid.

☐ I spent time alone just thinking about things.

☐ I drew a picture or diagram to aid me in communication
with others.

Seven Pathways of Learning © 1994 Zephyr Press, Tucson, Arizona

Teacher's Personal Reflection Log

SELF BEHAVIOR CHECKLIST

I have the following thoughts/insights about the Self Behavior Checklist strategy:

I feel that the Self Behavior Checklist strategy can help me in my teaching in the following ways:

As a learning process, the Self Behavior Checklist strategy includes the following benefits for my students:

I have the following specific ideas for using the Self Behavior Checklist strategy in my classroom in the near future:

I think the Self Behavior Checklist strategy can be used beyond the classroom and school in the following ways:

NOTES TO PARENTS

The Tacit Level of the Seven Ways of Knowing

The main goal of working with what I have called the tacit level of children's intelligence is to help them become aware that they do in fact have different ways of knowing and learning. It is important that children learn that we are not all the same.

Some children have unique and unorthodox ways of approaching a problem or dealing with a challenge. Sometimes these methods or strategies make one child seem strange to other children. Children may not understand or appreciate why one person may need to draw pictures to express what he or she is trying to say, for example, while another needs to act something out to really understand. Children who learn in these ways are not stupid or weird; we all have many different ways of knowing, understanding, learning, perceiving, and communicating with each other.

The five lessons presented in this chapter are examples of activities I suggest teachers incorporate into their daily teaching to help students become aware of and to appreciate the differences among them. The lessons are designed to help children become aware of the many highly intelligent things they do everyday, usually without thinking, and definitely without labeling the actions "intelligent behaviors." Once children can label some of these activities "intelligent," they often get a whole new image of themselves and of others.

I feel that this new and expanded self-concept is extremely important, especially for students who are not doing well in school. We are often too quick to attach various labels to students who have trouble learning through the verbal/linguistic and logical/mathematical modes, which comprise most of the teaching methods in schools today. Many times students' difficulties have nothing to do with so-called learning disabilities, but rather with learning differences, ways of knowing, learning, and understanding that our schools have not tapped. Helping children become aware of these differences not only makes a huge difference in their self-esteem, but it makes a difference in how they feel about each other as well. Billy's story at the beginning of this chapter is only one illustration of this increased peer respect.

The seven ways of knowing are related to the five senses, and all are inherent in the human brain. There are things you can do to trigger and nurture these different ways of knowing at home, in yourself and your children. In many ways doing so is a matter of awakening the full intelligence potential we already possess. Following are some suggestions that you can use at home to help your children tap each of the seven ways of knowing. These suggested activities and exercises are part of the tacit

Seven Pathways of Learning © 1994 Zephyr Press, Tucson, Arizona

level of intelligence described in the first paragraphs of this special parents' section. As you use these suggestions, make sure that you ask your children to be aware of the skills or capacities they are using.

Activities to Support the Tacit Use of the Intelligences

Verbal/Linguistic

* Play word games that involve understanding the order and meaning of words: Scrabble™, jumbles, crossword puzzles, Wheel of Fortune™, hangman.

* Have your child explain to you or teach you something she has learned.

* Tell each other jokes and teach your child about puns.

* Play memory games: any trivia game, vocabulary flash cards.

* Read and tell stories to each other.

* Get a book of limericks and read them to each other, then make up some of your own.

Logical/Mathematical

* Play guessing games that involve logical thinking: Clue™, Jeopardy™.

* Play games that require seeing patterns: Rummy Cube™.

* Play games that involve the development of a strategy to win: Monopoly™, Battleship™, checkers, tic-tac-toe.

* Brainstorm a list of possible solutions to a family problem, then prioritize the list.

* Play guess the pattern of, for example, a sequence of numbers, a grouping of objects, a set of words, a list of people or places.

Visual/Spatial

* Play games that require the use of visual skills: Pictionary™.

* Play "I'm thinking of something and its color or shape is . . . "

* Practice doing something in your imagination before you do it, such as a piano recital or a sports activity.

* Make up a story in which members of your family are the heroes, and draw pictures to illustrate it.

* Ask your child to draw images or symbols, including colors, to express his feelings.

* Play blindfold games: lead each other around blindfolded and guess where you are, Pin the Tail on the Donkey.

Bodily/Kinesthetic

* Play games that require physical movement and the use of the body: Twister™, charades.

* Learn sign language together.

* Learn and teach each other different kinds of dances.

* Make up a dance or drama about your family's history.

* Create a family exercise routine that you do together.

* Role-play a problem you are facing as a family, trying out a variety of solutions.

* Make a list of the body language family members use to express themselves and their feelings.

Seven Pathways of Learning © 1994 Zephyr Press, Tucson, Arizona

Activities to Support the Tacit Use of the Intelligences

(continued)

Musical/Rhythmic

★ Make a list of the different kinds of music family members like at different times of the day.

★ Write a song about your family using a popular tune.

★ Play music recognition games: Name that Tune™.

★ Discuss the use of music in TV shows, such as to create tension in detective stories or to signal that something funny is about to happen.

★ Learn songs and sing them together: popular songs, Christmas carols, Broadway tunes, religious songs.

★ Put certain family rules to music and rehearse them by singing the song.

★ List the sounds each member of the family makes to express him- or herself at different times and in different situations.

Intrapersonal

★ Play games that require you to focus mentally: Concentration™, card games such as go fish or hearts.

★ Have your child tell you how she approached a homework assignment.

★ Have each family member keep a daily journal or diary of her or his thoughts and feelings; give time each week for people to share what they want to.

★ Have each family member create a personal emblem or symbol, then tell the rest of the family about it.

★ Practice "watching yourself" doing routine things: washing dishes, cleaning, homework, and so on.

Interpersonal

★ Play various communication games: Gossip.

★ Create a family project in which each member has a part to complete.

★ Role-play what to do when there is a disagreement in the family.

★ Give each other supportive and clarifying feedback on some personal achievement or goal.

★ Teach and practice giving positive encouragement to each member of the family.

★ After watching a TV show or movie, see if you can guess what each member of the family thought about it.

=== 2 ===
Activities for Aware
Use of the Intelligences

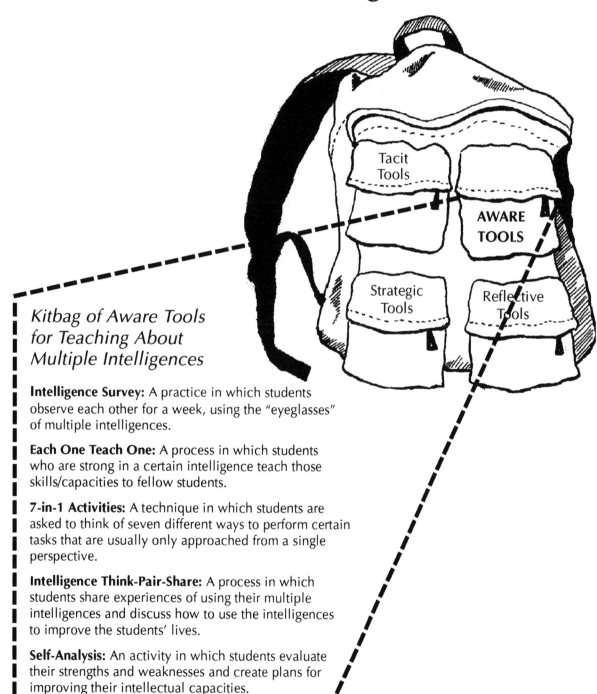

Tacit
Tools

AWARE
TOOLS

Strategic
Tools

Reflective
Tools

*Kitbag of Aware Tools
for Teaching About
Multiple Intelligences*

Intelligence Survey: A practice in which students observe each other for a week, using the "eyeglasses" of multiple intelligences.

Each One Teach One: A process in which students who are strong in a certain intelligence teach those skills/capacities to fellow students.

7-in-1 Activities: A technique in which students are asked to think of seven different ways to perform certain tasks that are usually only approached from a single perspective.

Intelligence Think-Pair-Share: A process in which students share experiences of using their multiple intelligences and discuss how to use the intelligences to improve the students' lives.

Self-Analysis: An activity in which students evaluate their strengths and weaknesses and create plans for improving their intellectual capacities.

Sandra was a middle school student. During the past year her teacher had been teaching the class about multiple intelligences. Sandra was intrigued with the idea that she has multiple ways of knowing but was hesitant to try using those at which she wasn't very skilled. She was afraid that other students would laugh at her.

The teacher was working with the students to help them learn how to improve and strengthen all of their ways of knowing. He created a list of skills for the different intelligences. The assignment was for each student to choose an intelligence in which she or he felt confident. In groups, the students were to create a plan and an activity that would help to strengthen the skills of the rest of the class. Sandra was pleased that she would get a chance to work in an intelligence area with which she was comfortable, but she was also excited that she would have an opportunity to practice using other intelligence skills in a safe environment where everyone was learning and trying new things.

When the groups had completed their planning, each group reported to the class by demonstrating their skills and the practice activity they had designed. The teacher set aside a brief time each day for students to practice one or two of the intelligences. The expert groups led the class in the practice sessions.

After two weeks, the teacher asked the class to discuss their feelings about the intelligence practice sessions. Sandra was one of the first to respond: "When I was asked to do things I'm not very good at, I was scared and uncomfortable at first. But when I saw that others also weren't good at all the skills, I was able to relax and get into it a little. I'm still not very good at the body stuff and the drawing, but at least I'm not afraid to try anymore!"

During the quarter, the practice sessions continued and students were pleased to notice that their skills in using the seven intelligences had definitely improved and that they felt more "at home" trying to use the skills to enhance learning.

☆　☆　☆

INTELLIGENCE SURVEY

Lesson Procedures

1. Group students into observation teams of three. Tell them they will be working with their teams for a week to observe teachers and other students in their class, and in the school as a whole, using the seven intelligences. Following is a list of what you and your students will be doing:

    - Use the "Intelligence Survey Checklists" (see examples, pp. 66–68), or even better, create your own checklist with the students. Students are to observe their fellow students and their teachers for a week and log each instance of the behaviors they see.
    - To log an instance, students are to go up to someone they see manifesting one of the behaviors on the checklist and say, "I caught you using your _____ intelligence!"
    - The students have that person sign his or her name on the intelligent behavior checklist.
    - At the end of the week you will tally the observation logs and create a bar graph. You want to find out which intelligent behaviors seem to occur more often than others and why.

2. Ask if all students understand the assignment. The first task of the team is to plan its observation strategy; for example, the team might decide to divide up the intelligences so that each person is specializing in looking for behaviors for two or three intelligences, or team members may want to assign each other various territories and groups of the school to cover.

3. Each day during the week give students a few minutes to share stories from their observations, to handle any difficulties they are experiencing, and to ask you any questions they may have.

Intelligence Survey

INTRODUCTION

This strategy is designed to help students appreciate the differences that exist among us in our various ways of knowing. It is designed also to give students a set of eyeglasses for seeing intelligence skills in others so that the students might learn to broaden their own perspectives when approaching an issue, challenge, or problem.

OBJECTIVE

The goal of this lesson is to help students recognize, first in others and then in themselves, different intelligences as those intelligences manifest themselves in the course of daily living.

DISCUSSION

This strategy is obviously not only beneficial to the students who are conducting the survey; it also makes other students aware and interested in the seven intelligences. The strategy involves taking small risks, but if you can get your students to try it even a couple of times they will start to have a great deal of fun with the exercise and will learn an immense amount. Not only must they recognize the intelligences in others, but they will have to explain the seven ways of knowing as well. Before students begin the survey, it would be a good idea for you to discuss with them what they should say when someone asks them about the intelligences.

4. At the end of the week, have each team tally the numbers for each behavior on the checklist. After the teams have their numbers, create a master tally of the numbers from all of the teams.

5. Use the following questions to lead the students in a discussion:

   - *What immediately grabs your attention as you look at these numbers?*
   - *What do you find surprising? Confusing? Exciting? Disturbing?*
   - *Why do you think these were the results?*
   - *What factors might have produced different results?*
   - *What have you learned about your own intelligences by doing this survey?*
   - *What new ideas did you get for how you might use all the ways of knowing in your schoolwork?*

6. Get one volunteer from each group to work as part of a team. The team will create a bar graph that shows the composite results of the survey. Have the team be imaginative and create something that you can display for the rest of the school to see.

Intelligence Survey Extensions

More Intelligence Survey Lesson Ideas

The following are ideas you may adapt to your academic content.

- **Special Groups Surveys.** Create a survey that students can use to analyze the different ways of knowing for groups of which they are a part. Some questions might include, "How are meetings run?" "Does the group have a symbol or an emblem? A song?" "What do members like to do for celebrations?" "How do they handle disagreements?" Each student is to pick five such groups, observe them over one month, and report the findings to the class.

- **Specific Capacities Surveys.** Design a survey around the specific capacities or skills of each intelligence. (See Capacities Inventory Wheel on p. 21.) Ask students to name people they know in the larger community who exhibit strength in particular intelligence areas: artists, actors, athletes, counselors, writers, computer programmers, bankers, and musicians. Assign students to survey two or three such people and report the findings to the class.

- **Cross-Culture Surveys.** Make up a survey for analyzing different cultural or ethnic groups. The survey could be created around things that reveal similarities and differences in how cultures use the seven ways of knowing to approach life: the importance of music, the kinds of visual art and its role in the culture, the nature

of interpersonal relationships (family, peer, social), the knowledge and enjoyment of folk dances, the spiritual or religious practices, and so on.

- **Male or Female Surveys.** Invent a survey around such things as how people process information, solve problems, and meet challenges in their daily lives. Assign students to interview ten men and ten women to see what specific differences the students can discover in how each gender group uses the seven ways of knowing.

- **Historical Surveys.** Create a survey for examining past periods of history using the seven intelligences. Ask students to analyze various periods to get a glimpse of differing emphases people in the eras placed on the seven intelligences: Ancient Greece, Middle Ages, or the United States during the Revolutionary War or during the "Great Awakening."

- **Family Surveys.** Assign students to interview members of their immediate families to see what the students can learn about how the seven intelligences have shaped their families. The interview or survey should be based on the seven ways of knowing and could include such questions as, "Who plays musical instruments?" "Who writes poetry?" "Who is really good at mathematical problem solving?" "Who likes to dance?" "Who is good at sports?" and so on.

Intelligence Survey Checklist
(Elementary)

I'm looking for . . .

1. **Someone who "talks" with her or his body.**

2. **Someone who is drawing.**

3. **Someone who is singing or humming as he or she works.**

4. **Someone who is talking to other people.**

5. **Someone who is alone and thinking.**

6. **Someone who is using numbers.**

7. **Someone who is reading or writing.**

Seven Pathways of Learning © 1994 Zephyr Press, Tucson, Arizona

Intelligence Survey Checklist
(Middle School)

Try to catch someone . . .

1. Having a good discussion with someone else.

2. Using body language to express her- or himself.

3. Humming or singing while doing something else.

4. Drawing pictures or images to communicate.

5. Trying to solve a problem.

6. Making a "speech" to convince others he or she is right about an idea.

7. Being alone and appearing to be deep in thought.

8. Giving directions to someone else for getting some place.

9. Taking notes on something (not in a classroom!).

10. Listening to music as he or she works or exercises.

11. Arguing.

12. Using math to solve an everyday, real-life problem.

13. Showing someone else how to do something through body movement.

14. Expressing "inner feelings" about something.

Seven Pathways of Learning © 1994 Zephyr Press, Tucson, Arizona

Intelligence Survey Checklist
(Secondary)

*How many of these behaviors
can you find in other people?*

1. Two or three people are talking and "good listening" is clearly going on.

2. Someone is expressing her- or himself through gestures and physical movement.

3. The tone of someone's voice is communicating how he or she feels about something (maybe even more than *what* he or she is saying!).

4. Someone is giving someone else directions to get somewhere (maybe drawing a map, as well!).

5. Someone is using metaphors, similes, and analogies to communicate ideas.

6. Someone is analyzing or evaluating the thinking patterns she or he used to make a recent decision.

7. Someone is using mathematical concepts to solve an everyday problem.

8. Someone is giving someone else positive support, encouragement, or feedback.

9. Someone is expressing ideas, opinions, or concepts through drawing (or any kind of visual media).

10. People are telling jokes or stories or debating an idea with one another.

11. Someone is using music as a background for some task he or she is trying to perform.

12. Someone is "acting out" his or her feelings, ideas, or opinions on some topic.

13. Someone has written a letter, poem, or an essay on a topic she or he feels strongly about.

14. People are sharing their problem-solving strategies (including creative approaches to homework!) with one another.

15. People are expressing their religious views, their thoughts on the "meaning of life," or sharing their feelings about themselves.

16. Someone is expressing her- or himself through a song, rap, or a rhythmic pattern.

17. Someone's walk or posture catches your attention and you sense it is communicating something about how that person is feeling.

Seven Pathways of Learning © 1994 Zephyr Press, Tucson, Arizona

Teacher's Personal Reflection Log

INTELLIGENCE SURVEY

I have the following thoughts/insights about the Intelligence Survey strategy:

I feel that the Intelligence Survey strategy can help me in my teaching in the following ways:

As a learning process, the Intelligence Survey strategy includes the following benefits for my students:

I have the following specific ideas for using the Intelligence Survey strategy in my classroom in the near future:

I think the Intelligence Survey strategy can be used beyond the classroom and school in the following ways:

Each One Teach One

INTRODUCTION

This lesson focuses on students helping each other learn specific skills that will enable the students to use all the intelligences more comfortably in the classroom. Current educational research shows that when peers teach something to peers, the learning often increases dramatically.

OBJECTIVE

The goal of the lesson is to expand students' intelligence skill base and to make them aware that intelligence can be practiced, improved, and fun.

DISCUSSION

The Each-One-Teach-One process is a very powerful learning strategy. William Glasser (1986), the renowned educational researcher, has stated that we learn approximately 10 percent of what we read, 20 percent of what we hear, 30 percent of what we see, 50 percent of what we see and hear, 70 percent of what we discuss with others, 80 percent of what we experience personally, and 95 percent of what we *teach* to someone else. In using this process, students not only reinforce and deepen their own skills, they also help fellow students hear, see, discuss, and experience the seven ways of knowing, thus learning how to use the full spectrum of their intellectual capabilities.

EACH ONE TEACH ONE

Lesson Procedures

1. Review the Multiple Intelligences Capacities Inventory Wheel included in the introduction. Remind the class of the various skills and capacities that are part of each intelligence.

2. Have students spend a few minutes thinking individually about how they feel about the seven intelligences. Post the following statements on an overhead or the board and have students complete each of the statements, selecting things from the examples. Remind students to consider all of the intelligences when they complete these sentences. Encourage them to venture beyond the safety of verbal/linguistic and logical/mathematical intelligences.

   - Three things I know how to do and am good at are . . .
   - Three things I don't like to do and am not very good at are . . .
   - Three things I would like to learn how to do better are . . .

3. Have each student place an asterisk by the item in the first list that is the capacity she or he knows how to do best or enjoys doing the most. Have her or him place another asterisk by the item in the third list that she or he most wants to learn.

4. Pass out two index cards to each student and have the students write their strongest or favorite capacity on one card and the capacity they want to learn on the other.

5. Divide the class into two sections. Ask one half to tape the want-to-learn cards to their chests, and ask the other half to tape the know-how-to-do cards to their chests. Have each half of the class sort itself into intelligence groups with others who have chosen "want-to-learn" or "know-how-to-do" capacities from the same intelligence.

6. Have the want-to-know and the know-how-to-do groups for each intelligence get together. Students in the know-how-to-do group are to teach the want-to-know skills to as many students as possible in the allotted time. Suggest that students use the following pattern to teach the skills:

   - Demonstrate the skill.
   - List the steps involved in performing the skill.
   - Go through one step at a time, helping the learners succeed at each step.
   - Put all the steps together.
   - Tell the learners several simple things they can do to practice the skill.

7. After a reasonable amount of time, have the class return to the two groups they formed in step 5. Have them switch roles: the second group tapes their want-to-know cards to their chests and the first group tapes their know-how-to-do cards to their chests. The first group now teaches the second group. You may have to do this part of the lesson on another day, depending on the amount of time you can give to the exercise.

8. After all students have had the opportunity to experience both roles, call the class back together and lead them in a discussion based on the following questions:

   - *What was this exercise like for you? What happened?*
   - *Which role did you like best—learner or teacher? Why?*
   - *What new discoveries did you make?*
   - *What new ideas did you get for improving your intelligences, especially those in which you feel weak?*
   - *What would have to happen in the classroom to encourage you to practice and use all of your intelligences every day? What things need to change?*

Each-One-Teach-One Extensions

More Each-One-Teach-One Lesson Ideas

The following are ideas you may adapt to your academic content.

- **Intelligence Skill-Building Tutorials.** For seven weeks, focus on teaching students the specific capacities or skills of one intelligence a week. Each day teach a new skill using the transfer model of instruction (see the introduction). Have students practice using the skill in learning and processing the day's academic content.

- **Intelligence Apprentice Projects.** Place students in groups, with one student who exhibits definite strength in a particular intelligence in each group. Place others in the group who want to develop their own skills in that area. Give the group an academic project to complete in which they must use the particular intelligence to the hilt. The "master" or "expert" in the intelligence is to train and work with the "apprentices" to produce the product.

- **Grade-Level Exchange Program.** At least once a week have children from the upper grades come to lower-grade classes to help the younger children develop their seven intelligences. Put four or five younger students in groups with two older students. Target specific skills for each training session and coach upper-grade students in specific activities to help them teach the skills.

- **Family Intelligence Training.** Assign students the task of teaching their families about the seven intelligences. Warn parents about this assignment so they are not caught off guard, and ask for their cooperation. Help the students learn how to explain the concept of "seven ways of knowing" and then brainstorm with them at least one experiential exercise for each intelligence they could use at home.

- **Intelligence Skill Relays.** Students work in teams of five and are paired with another team. Each member of the team draws an intelligence skill from a hat. The team then learns the set of skills its members have drawn. The first team sends one member to the second team to teach the skill. When the second team has performed the skill to the satisfaction of the first team, reverse the process. Continue the relay until each person has performed and taught his or her skill to the other team.

- **Seven-Ways-of-Knowing Videos.** Create a video presentation to inform parents or other classes about the seven ways of knowing. Work with students to write a script that explains the seven intelligences. Brainstorm ideas and decide on a demonstration or exercise that illustrates what it is like to use the seven intelligences in school. Film the demonstration or exercise.

Seven Pathways of Learning © 1994 Zephyr Press, Tucson, Arizona

Examples of Each-One-Teach-One Tasks
(Elementary)

Verbal/Linguistic
- tell a story
- write words/sentences
- read a sentence/paragraph

Logical/Mathematical
- count by twos
- solve a problem
- see/explain patterns

Visual/Spatial
- draw objects
- make shapes in clay
- read simple maps

Bodily/Kinesthetic
- understand gestures
- imitate body movement
- act out a feeling or scene

Musical/Rhythmic
- reproduce a tune or beat
- make expressive sounds
- recognize sounds

Interpersonal
- listen to a partner
- encourage others
- play social roles

Intrapersonal
- tell feelings
- name a goal
- tell who you are

Examples of Each-One-Teach-One Tasks
(Middle School)

Verbal/Linguistic
- make up and write a story
- tell a joke or understand a pun
- comprehend reading

Logical/Mathematical
- describe thinking patterns
- perform regular math operations
- understand math symbols

Visual/Spatial
- draw in perspective
- use accurate visual memory
- find a location on a map

Bodily/Kinesthetic
- teach a physical skill
- role-play or dance an idea
- play physical games

Musical/Rhythmic
- grasp music symbols
- be aware of different beats
- know musical sounds

Interpersonal
- be able to paraphrase
- take steps to build friendships
- take steps to develop empathy

Intrapersonal
- take steps to build self-esteem
- set personal goals
- be aware of likes and dislikes

Examples of Each-One-Teach-One Tasks
(Secondary)

Verbal/Linguistic
- be able to debate or speak on an issue
- write creatively (poetry/stories)
- understand figures of speech
- analyze language for meaning

Logical/Mathematical
- be aware of own thinking patterns
- make logical connections
- solve problems beyond school
- use math in everyday life

Visual/Spatial
- create unique art forms
- design things
- use complex internal imagery
- create accurate maps

Bodily/Kinesthetic
- show creative dramatic ability
- show creative dance ability
- be an inventor
- do a physical exercise routine

Musical/Rhythmic
- enjoy various forms of music
- express self in music
- perform music
- grasp music language

Interpersonal
- build consensus
- build cultural sensitivity
- show skill in group processes
- communicate well

Intrapersonal
- begin an identity quest
- establish a personal belief system
- control emotions
- understand symbols

Teacher's Personal Reflection Log

EACH-ONE-TEACH-ONE STRATEGY

I have the following thoughts/insights about the Each-One-Teach-One strategy:

I feel that the Each-One-Teach-One strategy can help me in my teaching in the following ways:

As a learning process, the Each-One-Teach-One strategy includes the following benefits for my students:

I have the following specific ideas for using the Each-One-Teach-One strategy in my classroom in the near future:

I think the Each-One-Teach-One strategy can be used beyond the classroom and school in the following ways:

76

7-IN-1 ACTIVITIES

Lesson Procedures

1. On the overhead or board write the following riddle:

   How many intelligences does it take to change a light bulb?

   Can you name them and tell how each would approach the task?

   Ask students to suggest strategies from each intelligence that would accomplish the task.

2. Tell your students, *"Anything and everything can be approached using the seven intelligences. All it takes is stretching your creativity a bit to figure out how. In this lesson you will have a chance to make this stretch!"*

3. Place students into groups of three or four. Pass out copies of the Multiple Intelligence Toolbox (pp. 80–81) to students. Say,

   The toolbox gives us strategies for using the seven intelligences. In this lesson your group will randomly select a topic from a set of cards (see pp. 82–84) for ideas). Your task is to choose one strategy from each intelligence that you think would help you learn about that topic. You are to record your ideas on a piece of newsprint so we can put them up on the wall and learn from your group's ideas.

4. Ask the groups if they have any questions about the assignment. Then take the stack of cards to each group and have one person draw a card. The topic on the card is the focus of the group's planning.

   If a group wants to draw another card because students can't figure out what to do with the card they got, allow them to do so. It is very important that you monitor the groups closely, helping them come up with ideas.

5. After the groups are finished with their planning, have each join two other groups and share their ideas. Then have each group post

7-in-1 Activities

INTRODUCTION

This lesson will help students learn to think about life and their school-work in new and more effective ways. It involves activating more intelligence capacities than one normally uses in any situation. Students will be asked to use all seven ways of knowing to deal with a single activity.

OBJECTIVE

The goal of the lesson is to help students get in touch with the well-springs of their own creativity by accessing and using all seven ways of knowing.

DISCUSSION

One of the most exciting and revealing ways to make students aware of the possibilities of the seven ways of knowing is through 7-in-1 activities. The essence of this lesson is to take specific concepts, ideas, or tasks and to force yourself to use all seven intelligences to deal with them. Possibly more than any other technique in this book, this one evokes the greatest creativity in students and provides them with a clear demonstration that learning can be a great deal of fun! While I believe that anything can be taught and learned in seven ways, it is probably best, at least initially, to have students deal with some of the topics in which the ways to apply the seven intelligences are more obvious.

its work in a part of the room set aside for the purpose.

6. Call the class back together and reflect on the lesson using the following questions:

- *What happened as you worked on this assignment? What things did you notice?*
- *What was easy? What was hard? What did you like? What did you not like?*
- *What surprised you? What excited you?*
- *In one sentence, how would you tell someone who was not here today what we did in this lesson?*
- *Think about lessons that we have done in the past week. What strategies could we have used that would have made the lessons better for you?*

7-in-1 Activities Extensions

More 7-in-1 Activities Lesson Ideas

The following are ideas you may adapt to your academic content.

- **Round Robin Intelligence.** Put students in groups of seven with each student representing one of the intelligences, preferably one he or she has chosen. Assign the groups to learn a particular concept from the lesson for the day using the seven ways of knowing. Each person in the group must help the others in the group learn the assigned material using the intelligence he or she is assigned.

- **Seven Ways of Knowing Party.** Work with students to plan a celebration around the theme of the seven intelligences. Have the students work in seven teams, each representing one of the intelligences. They are to create costumes for themselves that communicate the intelligence they are representing, an intelligence game for the rest of the class to play, a snack that represents their intelligence, and a decoration for the room.

- **Multidimensional Tasks.** Brainstorm a list of ordinary, mundane tasks that students must perform: making the bed, doing the dishes after dinner, cleaning their rooms, and so on. Have students get into groups of three or four. In some random way have them choose one of the tasks from the list. As a team they are to invent new ways to perform the task using all seven intelligences. When they are finished, have each team perform its task for the whole class.

- **Designing the MI School.** Group students in teams of five. They are to pretend that they are multiple intelligence architects whose task is to create a school environment that supports and nurtures the seven ways of knowing. They should consider such things as the decor, arrangement of space, supplies and materials, equipment, music, schedule, and so on. Each group is to draw the blueprint of what this new, multimodal school would look like.

- **Intelligence Games.** Have students get into seven groups, one for each intelligence. The groups make a list of games and puzzles that require the use of their assigned intelligence. Some examples include Scrabble™ for verbal/linguistic, Pictionary™ for visual/spatial, or hopscotch for bodily/kinesthetic. Each group then invents a new game that accesses the capacities or skills of its assigned intelligence. Over the next several weeks, allow each group to lead the class in playing its new game.

- **Illustrating a Story or Reading.** Break students into seven groups, one for each intelligence. Read them a story or article and have the groups brainstorm various ways that the story could be "illustrated" using the media appropriate to their assigned intelligence: sounds, music, and rhythm; colors, images, textures, and designs; physical gestures, movement, and dance; and so on. Read the story or article again, this time with each group showing or performing its "illustrations."

Verbal/Linguistic

- Reading
- Vocabulary
- Journal or diary keeping
- Creative writing
- Poetry
- Humor or telling jokes
- Storytelling

Logical/Mathematical

- Outlining
- Graphic organizers
- Number sequences
- Deciphering codes
- Problem solving
- Pattern games

Bodily/Kinesthetic

- Folk or creative dance
- Role-playing
- Physical gestures
- Drama
- Martial arts
- Body language
- Physical exercise
- Sports

Visual/Spatial

- Guided imagery
- Active imagination
- Color schemes
- Patterns and designs
- Painting
- Drawing
- Mind mapping
- Pretending
- Sculpture
- Pictures

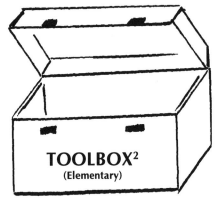

TOOLBOX²
(Elementary)

Interpersonal

- Giving feedback
- Intuiting others' feelings
- Cooperative learning strategies
- Person-to-person communication
- Empathy practices
- Division of labor
- Collaboration skills
- Receiving feedback
- Group projects

Intrapersonal

- Silent reflection methods
- Metacognition techniques
- Thinking strategies
- Emotional processing
- "Know thyself" practices
- Mindfulness practices
- Focusing and concentration skills
- "Centering" practices

Musical/Rhythmic

- Rhythmic patterns
- Humming
- Environmental sounds
- Instrumental sounds
- Singing
- Music performance

2. Adapted from Lazear, David. *Seven Ways of Knowing.* Palatine, Ill.: Skylight, 1991.

Verbal/Linguistic
- Reading
- Vocabulary
- Formal speech
- Journal or diary keeping
- Creative writing
- Poetry
- Oral debate
- Impromptu speaking
- Humor or telling jokes
- Storytelling

Logical/Mathematical
- Abstract symbols and formulas
- Outlining
- Graphic organizers
- Number sequences
- Calculation
- Deciphering codes
- Forcing relationships
- Syllogisms
- Problem solving
- Pattern games

Bodily/Kinesthetic
- Folk or creative dance
- Role-playing
- Physical gestures
- Drama
- Martial arts
- Body language
- Physical exercise
- Mime
- Inventing
- Sports

Visual/Spatial
- Guided imagery
- Active Imagination
- Color schemes
- Patterns and designs
- Painting
- Drawing
- Mind mapping
- Pretending
- Sculpture
- Pictures

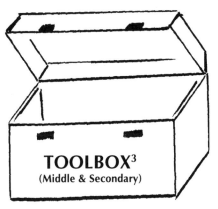

TOOLBOX³
(Middle & Secondary)

Musical/Rhythmic
- Rhythmic patterns
- Vocal sounds and tones
- Music composition and creation
- Percussion vibrations
- Humming
- Environmental sounds
- Instrumental sounds
- Singing
- Tonal patterns
- Music performance

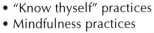

Intrapersonal
- Silent reflection methods
- Metacognition techniques
- Thinking strategies
- Emotional processing
- "Know thyself" practices
- Mindfulness practices
- Focusing and concentration skills
- Higher-order reasoning
- Complex guided imagery
- "Centering" practices

Interpersonal
- Giving feedback
- Intuiting others' feelings
- Cooperative learning strategies
- Person-to-person communication
- Empathy practices
- Division of labor
- Collaboration skills
- Receiving feedback
- Sensing others' motives
- Group projects

3. Adapted from Lazear, David. *Seven Ways of Knowing.* Palatine, Ill.: Skylight, 1991.

7-In-1 Activities
(Elementary)

Activity Cards

Tie your shoes.	**Brush your teeth.**
Pick up your room.	**Wash your face and hands.**
Care for a pet.	**Use good table manners.**

Seven Pathways of Learning © 1994 Zephyr Press, Tucson, Arizona

7-In-1 Activities
(Middle School)

Activity Cards

Meet people at a party.

Order food at McDonald's.

Shop for a new pair of shoes.

Make up after an argument.

Tell parents about your day.

Meet your friends at the mall.

7-In-1 Activities
(Secondary)

Activity Cards

Ask someone for a date.

Fill out a job application.

Think about college opportunities.

Tell a friend about a problem.

Plan a party with your friends.

Say "NO" to drugs in different ways.

Teacher's Personal Reflection Log

7-IN-1 ACTIVITIES

I have the following thoughts/insights about the 7-in-1 Activities strategy:

I feel that the 7-in-1 Activities strategy can help me in my teaching in the following ways:

As a learning process, the 7-in-1 Activities strategy includes the following benefits for my students:

I have the following specific ideas for using the 7-in-1 Activities strategy in my classroom in the near future:

I think the 7-in-1 Activities strategy can be used beyond the classroom and school in the following ways:

Intelligence Think-Pair-Share

INTRODUCTION

This lesson asks students to share their everyday experiences of using the seven ways of knowing to help each other find applications of the intelligences in their lives beyond school. The sharing will provide new insights and new ideas for all students regarding possible uses for the seven intelligences.

OBJECTIVE

The goal of the lesson is to allow students to exchange information regarding their intelligences and how the intelligences are part of everyday living.

DISCUSSION

This particular learning strategy is one of the best for teaching students the social skill of listening to another person. Having to paraphrase what their partners said is the acid test of whether they were really listening. After the first round of think-pair-share, brainstorm a list of ideas, based on this experience, that students could use to be better listeners. Then give them an opportunity to work with different partners and do the exercise again, this time trying to improve their listening by applying some of the suggestions from the list.

INTELLIGENCE THINK-PAIR-SHARE

Lesson Procedures

1. Project the grade-appropriate work sheet on an overhead or write it on the board (see pp. 89–91). Address each question in turn and give students a minute to think of an experience they have had or a time they used the particular intelligences implied in the questions. Have them make a few notes to themselves to use later in the lesson when they share their experiences with partners.

2. After you have been through all of the questions, have each student choose a partner, one that she or he doesn't know too well, not a good friend in the class.

3. Have the pairs decide who will be person A and who will be person B.

   - Person B quickly shares his or her list of times when he or she used the intelligences.
   - Person A listens carefully to what person B shares. When person B is finished, person A takes a few moments to ask person B questions or to ask for more details on anything person A found particularly interesting.
   - Now person A is to try to remember the seven things person B shared. Person B may coach person A.
   - Repeat the process with person A sharing and person B listening.

4. Have each pair join with another pair. Each person, in turn, is to share with the foursome what his or her partner shared in as much detail as he or she can remember. The former partners may amend and clarify as necessary.

5. After all four people have shared their partners' experiences with multiple intelligences, have each person write his or her answers to the following questions:

Seven Pathways of Learning © 1994 Zephyr Press, Tucson, Arizona

> • *How did hearing about others' experiences with multiple intelligences help you?*
> • *What new ideas for using the intelligences did you get from each other?*

6. After students have completed the think- pair-share as a foursome and have answered the discussion questions, pull the class back together and lead them in the following reflection:

> • *What was the most interesting thing you heard from someone else about how he or she uses or has used the multiple intelligences?*
> • *How does this kind of sharing make you feel? What did you like? Not like?*
> • *Ask several groups to share their answers to the two questions in number 5.*
> • *Quickly go around the class and have each person complete the sentence "One new intelligent thing I plan to try is . . ."*

Think-Pair-Share Extensions

More Intelligence Think-Pair-Share Lesson Ideas

The following are ideas you may adapt to your academic content.

• **Paraphrased Interviews.** Assign students to create questions for an interview based   on their use of and feelings about particular intelligences. After the interviews each student is to write a brief summary about what his or her partner said in the interview. Have students check the accuracy of their summaries with the appropriate partners.

• **Listening between the Lines.** Have each student find a partner that she or he does not know well. Each partner is to have "air time" to tell about an important event in his or her life: a family vacation, the birth of a baby brother or sister, and so on. As each person tells the story, the other is to listen to the verbal telling while "listening" to the nonverbal cues the teller uses: body language, voice tone and sounds, breathing patterns, emotions, and so on. The listener then tells what she or he "heard" in the nonverbal cues.

• **Multimedia Reporting.** Play an audio tape of a famous speech. Place students in groups of three or four and have them listen carefully to the tape and then create a multimodal report on what they heard; they may write newspaper headlines and a short article, create a picture or image to go along with the written report, choose a musical introduction or background music, make up appropriate body gestures or physical movements, or share the feelings the speech evoked.

- **Intelligence Communication Clues.** Give students a serious, short piece of poetry and have several read it to the class. Discuss how sometimes the way we say something communicates more than the words themselves. Have students turn to partners and experiment with changing the meaning of the poem through such things as tone of voice, body posture and gestures, facial expressions, and so on. For example, students might read as if they had just had a fight with a good friend, as if they were deeply in love, as if the poem were the script in a comedy nightclub, and so on.

- **Conversations from the Past.** Ask students to write the name of a historical or literary figure you have been studying. Have students choose partners and imagine they are the figures they listed. Assign them a question to discuss in character. After each has had a chance to role-play his or her character, have the pairs join other pairs. Each student will become his or her partner's character, saying and doing what the partner did in the previous discussion.

- **TPS at Home.** Assign students to try the think-pair-share strategy in various situations at home. Brainstorm a list of situations in which it might work: in a family discussion in which there are different points of view, as a way to debrief each other on the events of the day, or as a mediation strategy when there is disagreement are a few possibilities. After making the list, have students work in groups of three or four to help each other think of how they could adapt the list to each situation.

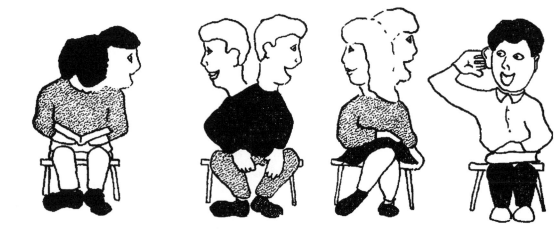

Seven Pathways of Learning © 1994 Zephyr Press, Tucson, Arizona

Think-Pair-Share
(Elementary)

Answer these questions:

1. **What do you like to read?**

2. **When do you use numbers?**

3. **What do you like to draw?**

4. **What games do you like to play?**

5. **What music do you like?**

6. **Do you like to talk to others?**

7. **What do you do when you're alone?**

Think-Pair-Share
(Middle School)

Can you think of a time when . . .

1. **You read something outside of school that was really interesting to you?**

2. **You used math to help you in your everyday life?**

3. **You drew something to help you communicate with someone else?**

4. **You played a game in which you used your body a lot?**

5. **You listened to music to help you relax or to help you be more creative?**

6. **You asked a friend for advice on a personal problem or challenge you were facing?**

7. **You spent some time alone just thinking?**

Seven Pathways of Learning © 1994 Zephyr Press, Tucson, Arizona

Think-Pair-Share

(Secondary)

When have you experienced the following situations?

1. **You read something that was important or meaningful to you and you discussed it with someone else.**

2. **You used math concepts or processes to help you solve a problem in your everyday life.**

3. **You used drawing, painting, or sculpture to express something you were feeling or thinking.**

4. **You used body language, physical gestures, or role-playing to help you communicate.**

5. **You used music to change how you were feeling or to improve your performance in an activity.**

6. **You were part of a successful team and could talk about the factors that contributed to its success.**

7. **You learned something new about yourself: how you think, how you feel, what you believe, or what you think is really important.**

Teacher's Personal Reflection Log

INTELLIGENCE THINK-PAIR-SHARE

I have the following thoughts/insights about the Intelligence Think-Pair-Share strategy:

I feel that the Intelligence Think-Pair-Share strategy can help me in my teaching in the following ways:

As a learning process, the Intelligence Think-Pair-Share strategy includes the following benefits for my students:

I have the following specific ideas for using the Intelligence Think-Pair-Share strategy in my classroom in the near future:

I think the Intelligence Think-Pair-Share strategy can be used beyond the classroom and school in the following ways:

SELF-ANALYSIS

Lesson Procedures

1. Tell students that in this lesson they will analyze the relative strengths and weaknesses of their own seven ways of knowing. The first part of the lesson is an individual task.

2. Project the appropriate self-analysis chart from the examples (pp. 97–99) on the overhead or draw it on the board. Have students reproduce the chart on a piece of blank paper. They will analyze their intelligences. Ask students to do their analyses in silence, trying to be as honest as they can about their feelings. Encourage them to trust their first instinct or to go with their first impression of what their responses should be. Now explain how it works:

   - **Elementary.** For each question on the chart, have students draw the face that expresses how they feel about the question. If they need to draw a different face from those at the top of the chart, they may.

   - **Middle.** For each way of knowing, there are three items listed. In the columns at the far right, have students rank themselves based on how much they like to do and how good they are at each component. They will use the plus and minus scale at the top of the page as their ranking guide. Each of the twenty-one items should have a mark beside it when the students are finished.

   - **Secondary.** Students will evaluate how well they use the skills or capacities listed under each of the seven intelligences. The students will use the scale at the top of the page as a guide. Each item should have a number between 0 and 10 beside it. When students have answered each of the questions, they will total the numbers by each intelligence and place the figure in the column at the right.

Self-Analysis

INTRODUCTION

In this lesson students have an opportunity to take a good look at themselves and to evaluate their intelligence strengths and weaknesses. Students will also create an initial plan for improving any weaknesses they discover.

OBJECTIVES

The goal of this lesson is to provide students with a chance to get to know themselves and their intelligences better. It also helps them discover that they can be proactive in the development of their intelligence capacities.

DISCUSSION

The trick to being successful with this strategy is to get students to be honest in their analysis of themselves. One of the keys to achieving this honesty is to make sure they understand that the analysis contains no judgments of good or bad. We are all strong in certain intelligences and weak in others. The good news about doing this kind of self-analysis is that as soon as we are aware of certain strengths and weaknesses, we can capitalize on the strengths and work to improve the weaknesses.

3. Now have each student turn to a partner and compare his or her responses with that partner's. Have students ask themselves the following questions:

   - *What immediately strikes you as you look at your charts?*
   - *What surprises you? Intrigues you? Bothers you? Confuses you? Pleases you?*
   - *What does this activity tell you about yourself?*

4. Have students make two lists with their partners:

   - *List at least five things you can do to capitalize on and use your own intelligence strengths more fully in your daily classroom work.*
   - *List at least five things you can do to stretch your intelligence weaknesses to create a greater balance and use all seven ways of knowing.*

5. Call the class back together and lead them in a brief general discussion using the following. Ask for several volunteers to share what happened.

   - *What did you discover as you did your self-analysis?*
   - *What are some of the ideas you and your partner thought of to help you use your stronger intelligences more?*
   - *What are some ideas you had for stretching your weaknesses?*
   - *How can we use this information to help us create a more interesting classroom where we are using all intelligences for teaching and learning? Make a list of ideas on a piece of newsprint.*

Seven Pathways of Learning © 1994 Zephyr Press, Tucson, Arizona

You might consider having students choose something each day from their lists to try and implement while they are in your class, on the school grounds, or in the cafeteria with their friends.

Self-Analysis Extensions

More Self-Analysis Lesson Ideas

The following are ideas you may adapt to your academic content.

- **Intelligence Instant Replay.** Ask students to make individual lists of at least three recent situations in which they were required to make a decision. Have them reconsider each decision from the perspective of the seven intelligences, pretending they can do an instant replay of the decision. Ask the students to change anything in the instant replay that occurs to them as they think about the seven intelligences. After they work alone, have them share with a partner to get additional suggestions.

- **Intelligence Safari.** Ask students to set aside a place in their notebooks for tracking their use of the seven ways of knowing. Choose three consecutive weeks and assign students the task of "stalking" their intelligences; that is, they are to list the intelligences they were most aware of using during the day, including descriptions of when and where they used the intelligences. At the end of each week have students hunt for a weekly pattern: Which intelligences did they use most? least? Have students create a plan for using more intelligences each day of the next week.

- **Your Intelligence Comfort Zones.** After completing a lesson in which you used the seven ways of knowing or one of the seven, have students rank themselves on a continuum regarding the affective aspects of the different intelligences; students may write anything from "I felt like a fish in water" to "I felt like I had landed on another planet." Then have students turn to partners and compare rankings, discussing why they responded in the ways they did.

- **Translating Intelligence Strengths.** Pass out one index card to each student. Have students write on their cards the intelligence that they feel is their strongest. Have them list on the back of the cards areas in school, nonacademic as well as academic, in which they have trouble. Have each student pair with another who has the same strength on the front of his or her card. Have the pairs work together to figure out how to use the strong intelligence to deal with the trouble areas listed on the backs of their cards.

- **Multimodal Communication.** Have each student make a list of recent experiences when he or she tried to communicate an idea or thought. Ask the students to analyze how the effectiveness of their communication could have been improved if they had used the seven intelligences: using "visuals," appropriate body language and gestures, variations of voice tone and pitch and other sounds, and so on. Now have them find partners and replay their earlier communication, incorporating some of their ideas.

- **The Homework Connection.** Ask each student to list all of the homework assignments he or she can remember from the past week. Next have students name the intelligence that was predominant. Then ask them to go back through the list and write down ideas of the intelligences they could have employed that would have made the homework more interesting, fun, easy, or that might have helped them learn more.

Seven Pathways of Learning © 1994 Zephyr Press, Tucson, Arizona

Self-Analysis
(Elementary)

What Do I Like?	
🙂 🙁 😐	
Reading and writing	
Working with numbers	
Drawing and painting	
Body stuff	
Singing	
Working with others	
Being alone	

Self-Analysis
(Middle School)

What do I like and what am I good at?		
+++ = "super!" − − − = "ugh!" ++ = "okay" − − = "fair" + = "so, so" − = "so, so"	**Pluses**	**Minuses**
Verbal/Linguistic: reading writing speaking		
Logical/Mathematical: working with numbers solving problems thinking logically		
Visual/Spatial: pretending and using the imagination drawing/painting/working with clay finding my way		
Bodily/Kinesthetic: playing roles playing physical games exercising my body		
Musical/Rhythmic: singing or playing music sounding rhythm or beats recognizing different sounds		
Interpersonal: listening to others encouraging and supporting others being part of a team		
Intrapersonal: talking positively to myself being aware of my feelings liking to do some things alone		

Seven Pathways of Learning © 1994 Zephyr Press, Tucson, Arizona

Self-Analysis
(Secondary)

What am I good at?			
10 = *WOW!* 10 9 8 7 6 5 4 3 2 1 0 *0 = UGH!*			
		Individual Capacity Ranking	**Totals**
Verbal/Linguistic: 1. Reading and understanding what I've read 2. Communicating through writing something I'm thinking 3. Making a speech or giving a report			
Logical/Mathematical: 1. Doing math in my head 2. Knowing that I've received the correct change at the store 3. Figuring out how to solve everyday problems			
Visual/Spatial: 1. Finding my way using a map 2. Drawing an object or scene on paper 3. Pretending or imagining things			
Bodily/Kinesthetic: 1. Playing charades or roles (as in drama) 2. Dancing or playing games that require body movement 3. Exercising my body for better body performance			
Musical/Rhythmic: 1. Being able to hum a tune I've heard on the radio or a tape 2. Recognizing different recorded instruments and sounds 3. Using music to alter my feelings and moods			
Interpersonal: 1. Listening to others' opinions and feelings (even when I disagree) 2. Doing my part when I'm part of a team project 3. Giving encouragement and positive support to other people			
Intrapersonal: 1. Spending time alone thinking things through 2. Being aware of and dealing with my own feelings 3. Evaluating my own thinking patterns and improving them			

Teacher's Personal Reflection Log

SELF-ANALYSIS

I have the following thoughts/insights about the Self-Analysis strategy:

I feel that the Self-Analysis strategy can help me in my teaching in the following ways:

As a learning process, the Self-Analysis strategy includes the following benefits for my students:

I have the following specific ideas for using the Self-Analysis strategy in my classroom in the near future:

I think the Self-Analysis strategy can be used beyond the classroom and school in the following ways:

Seven Pathways of Learning © 1994 Zephyr Press, Tucson, Arizona

NOTES TO PARENTS

The Aware Level of the Seven Ways of Knowing

The goal of the aware level of learning about the seven ways of knowing is to help children learn how the different intelligences work. I am concerned that children know what is involved in using their seven intelligences, what the various capacities and skills are, how the children can access or trigger those skills, and what some of the possibilities are for using the different ways of knowing every day.

As students work at this level they discover immediately that, while we all possess all seven ways of knowing, not all of our intelligences are of the same strength. In fact, most of us feel comfortable with or somewhat skillful in one or two of the areas, and much less comfortable with and somewhat unskilled in others. This discovery is not a reason for discouragement, however. Since the intelligences are part of our neurology and physiology as human creatures, we can strengthen a weakness through practice. In fact, the intelligences are very much like any skill we have; the more we practice it, the better we can do it, whether it is swinging a golf club, parking a car, cooking, or building something.

As we saw at the tacit level, each of the intelligences is related to the five senses and can be activated or triggered through exercises that stimulate the senses of sight, sound, taste, touch, and smell, as well as speech. We can also use the inner senses, such as intuition, metacognition, and spiritual insight, to trigger the intelligences. At the aware level we are concerned first with learning specific techniques and methodologies to enhance and strengthen the knowing and learning powers of an intelligence that has been triggered.

It's exercise only if you push the pedals!

The aware level of the intelligences also involves learning how to interpret and understand the different kinds of information we receive. We must learn the unique language, jargon, and vernacular of each intelligence, that is, how each expresses itself and how we can speak the language of the particular intelligence we want to use. For example, the "language" of musical/rhythmic intelligence is tones and rhythmic patterns—*not* words, sentences, writing, and speech. If we are to use the musical/rhythmic way of knowing effectively, we must learn to recognize and reproduce musical tones and rhythm patterns and to interpret the meaning of different sounds.

Practice in using the seven ways of knowing is the key to strengthening and improving them. The five lessons in this chapter are examples of the kinds of classroom practices I recommend. Following is a list of exercises that you might use at home to help your children enhance and strengthen the full range of their intelligence capabilities. Why not give some of the exercises a try and see what happens to you and your children? I promise that you can improve your intellectual skills if you consciously exercise them.

Seven Pathways of Learning © 1994 Zephyr Press, Tucson, Arizona

Activities to Support the Aware Use of the Intelligences

Verbal/Linguistic

★ Practice writing about a mundane event each day as if it were the central turning point of history. Use a lot of juicy, descriptive words, metaphors, and similes.

★ At dinner, choose a topic at random to discuss. Have each family member speak as if he or she were an expert on the topic.

★ Pick a new word at random from the dictionary each day, learn its meaning, and consciously try to use it in various conversations with other people throughout the day.

★ Debate the pros and cons of something from the evening news, making sure each person expresses her or his opinions.

★ Try joint storytelling. You begin telling a tale, stop at different points, and ask another person to continue the story.

Logical/Mathematical

★ Videotape a TV detective show. Watch the show, stopping the action at critical points and asking people to predict what will happen next. Continue the tape and check the predictions, analyzing the clues people missed that could have improved the accuracy of their predictions.

★ Make up a family code and leave notes written in the code for each other.

★ Choose a problem situation from the news, a situation comedy, or a soap opera, and brainstorm all the realistic solutions you can think of to solve the problem. Choose the "best" solution.

★ Have each family member create a four-point outline of one of his or her hobbies, with each point having four related subpoints, and each subpoint having four subpoints.

★ Create a numbers-at-the-dinner-table exercise: the number of fork prongs, the number of fingers not counting thumbs, the average number of helpings of food people take, and so on.

Visual/Spatial

★ Imagine seeing a place the family has visited or lived in. Each person describes what he or she is seeing and helps the others "see" aspects that they may have neglected.

★ Experiment with visual media (paints, clay, colored markers, collages) to express what your day was like or an idea you want to tell others.

★ Practice leading each other on various fantasy trips to exotic places and times. Ask people to imagine everything that is suggested in the journey.

★ Practice getting around by reading a map. Go to a place that you do not know well and get lost intentionally. Use a map to get back to a familiar spot.

Activities to Support the Aware Use of the Intelligences

(continued)

Bodily/Kinesthetic

★ Role-play or mime an idea, opinion, situation, or feeling using *only* body movement and physical gestures to communicate.

★ Go for a walk and practice walking in different ways to match certain moods or feelings: the thinking-things-over walk, the angry walk, the joyful or excited walk, the sad or depressed walk, the determined walk, and so on.

★ Several times during the day, practice "physical mindfulness." Choose some routine activity and perform it in slow motion, carefully observing the body in action.

★ Think of a challenge the family is facing. Is it like trying to blast through a brick wall, being caught in a spider web, or what? Think about the challenge and act out breaking through the wall, untangling yourself from the web, or whatever matches your image.

Musical/Rhythmic

★ Sit alone in several different environments and list every sound you hear. See if you can picture what is making the sound and what is going on.

★ Practice making certain sounds to express emotions: contentment, fear, anger, sadness, excitement, disappointment, and so on. Experiment with using these sounds to punctuate your conversations with others.

★ Decide which stages or periods of your family's history are major stages. Choose a piece of music to go with each stage. Listen to each piece, starting with the first stage and progressing through the last.

★ Experiment with different kinds of music and beats that enhance your performance during the day; for example, you might choose music to lower your stress level, to make you more creative, to make you happy, or to help you focus on a task.

★ Read or tell a story and create sounds, rhythms, music, beats, and other tonal patterns or noises to "illustrate" the story.

Activities to Support the Aware Use
of the Intelligences
(continued)

Intrapersonal

★ Practice the art of watching yourself as you become involved in different tasks. Imagine yourself as an outside observer of you, especially in situations that tend to throw you off balance.

★ Pretend that you have a personal coach or counselor inside your head, one who knows all about you and your needs. Practice going inside to talk with this person about how to reach your full human potential.

★ After any task you accomplish during the day, practice taking a few minutes to step back and evaluate your performance: "What did I do well?" and "Where do I need to improve?"

★ Experiment with keeping a mood chart or graph to track your feelings during the day or week. Note high points, low points, and middle-of-the-road points. Note what kinds of external things were happening at each point.

Interpersonal

★ Try to listen fully and completely to another person. Practice the discipline of cutting off the "mind chatter" that continually evaluates what others are saying, even before they've said it!

★ Practice disciplined people-watching and see how much you can learn and how attuned you can become to other people, their feelings, expressions, body language, tones of speech, and so on.

★ In talking with other people, practice extending their statements by asking relevant questions that help you understand where they are coming from. Get to know them and their thinking as much as you can.

★ Experiment with different ways to help a group improve its interpersonal skills: create a group motto, emblem, and cheer; list accomplishments on the wall; plan a celebration; discuss what's going well in the group and what needs to be improved.

3

Activities for Strategic Use of the Intelligences

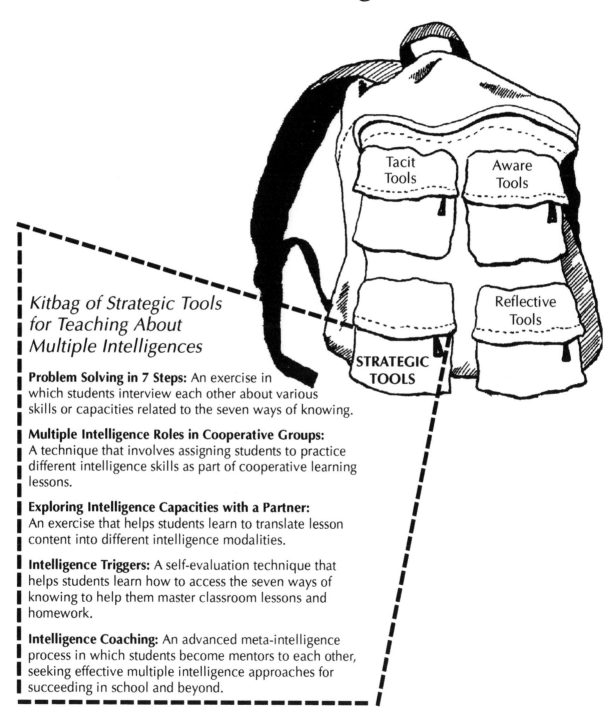

Kitbag of Strategic Tools for Teaching About Multiple Intelligences

Problem Solving in 7 Steps: An exercise in which students interview each other about various skills or capacities related to the seven ways of knowing.

Multiple Intelligence Roles in Cooperative Groups: A technique that involves assigning students to practice different intelligence skills as part of cooperative learning lessons.

Exploring Intelligence Capacities with a Partner: An exercise that helps students learn to translate lesson content into different intelligence modalities.

Intelligence Triggers: A self-evaluation technique that helps students learn how to access the seven ways of knowing to help them master classroom lessons and homework.

Intelligence Coaching: An advanced meta-intelligence process in which students become mentors to each other, seeking effective multiple intelligence approaches for succeeding in school and beyond.

I t was the day after the big unit test in Mr. Boggs's high school chemistry class. As a whole, the class had not done well. And it was doubly distressing to Mr. Boggs because the very students he thought understood the material best did poorest on the test. He decided to talk with the class and ask them what went wrong.

Some of the comments he got follow:

> *I don't know what went wrong. When we are in the lab and I can be doing chemistry, I understand it perfectly. It's when I have to write about it that I seem to lose it all.*

> *The test was fake. Where in real life would we ever have to go off by ourselves and answer a bunch of dumb ol' questions? In class we could talk to each other. We could ask you questions. We could relate. I know a lot more than I could show you on the test!*

> *Chemistry is seeing stuff happen, like when you mix things together and the solution changes color, or starts to smoke, or makes a bad smell. When you taught us you used all kinds of cool drawings to help us imagine what was going on in a chemical reaction. How come we couldn't draw on the test?*

These and other comments came like a bolt of lightning to Mr. Boggs. He had been using multiple intelligences to teach chemistry for some time and had discovered that students not only enjoyed his class more, but they seemed to understand the material better.

The tragic flaw was that he had expected them to make the transfer of learning suddenly from a full-blown "multi" intelligence teaching and learning situation to a "mono" intelligence paper-and-pencil test.

This experience caused Mr. Boggs to move in several new directions in his classroom. First, he started helping students develop bridging or transfer strategies for classroom activities in which the students were engaged. Second, he placed students in multiple intelligence coaching teams and gave them the written test again. This time, however, they were allowed to help each other "translate" the verbal/linguistic stuff into other intelligence modalities, which gave all the students a chance to win and use all their intelligences on the test itself. Third, on future tests Mr. Boggs offered a variety of ways from which students could choose to demonstrate what they knew; he also required everyone to use at least three different intelligences in addition to the verbal/linguistic.

Needless to say, all Mr. Boggs's students were much more successful on the next test, which made Mr. Boggs much happier.

★ ★ ★

PROBLEM SOLVING IN 7 STEPS

Lesson Procedures

1. Lead students in a preliminary discussion of what they usually do when they have a problem to solve.

   - Have each student list two to three problems he or she has solved recently. Get a random sampling of the kinds of problems the students listed.
   - Have them individually list the steps they went through to find a solution.
   - Have each student turn to a neighbor and compare and contrast problem-solving approaches.
   - On the overhead list some of the steps students used to solve problems. Try to get a cross-section of the variety of approaches different individuals used.

2. Place students into cooperative groups of three to four. Assign each group one of the problem scenarios from the examples (see pp.112-14). The students' task is to find seven different ways to approach solving their assigned problem. Have them figure out the intelligence-appropriate steps to use for solving the problem. Once they have mapped out these steps, have them role-play the situation using the intelligence steps they have created and see what happens.

   Make sure students know that they can do anything they want to find a solution. Also make sure that a wide variety of media are available for their use: colored markers, paints, clay, musical and percussion instruments, and so on. Remember that, in terms of the objective of this lesson, proposing creative solutions that use the seven intelligences is more important than finding the "right" answer.

3. Allow time for each team to share the variety of things they did to find a solution to their assigned problem.

Problem Solving in 7 Steps

INTRODUCTION

This lesson involves students in problem-solving tasks that bring all seven intelligences to bear on a single problem. When we use more of the brain's full intellectual potential on a single problem we can often find more and better solutions.

OBJECTIVE

The goal of the lesson is for students to learn how they can use the seven intelligences in any situation that presents a problem or a challenge and for them to discover that using all the intelligences creates a deeper, richer, and more varied approach to the task of living.

DISCUSSION

This strategy is a more complex version of the 7-in-1 Activities strategy in chapter 2. Problem Solving in 7 Steps involves learning to use the seven intelligences to amplify possibilities and options to solve problems and meet life's challenges. The same results can happen when all seven intelligences are brought to bear on the learning and processing of daily classroom material. While I am not suggesting that every lesson should be a "7-in-1" lesson, I believe that it is important that students (and teachers!) realize that *anything* and *everything* can be taught and learned in seven different ways. And the more levels on which a lesson is taught and learned, the more integrated the knowing and learning experience becomes for students.

4. After each team has given its report, lead your class in the following discussion of the lesson:

- *What happened as you tried to use all seven intelligences to solve a single problem?*

- *What happened to your understanding or perception of the problem?*

- *What was helpful to you? What was not helpful?*

- *What have you learned that you think can help you when you have everyday problems to solve or new challenges to meet?*

Problem Solving in 7 Steps Extensions

More Problem Solving in 7 Steps Lesson Ideas

The following are ideas you may adapt to your academic content.

- **School Issues Plan.** Make a list of students' issues or concerns about their school and education. Place students in groups of three to four, assigning each group one issue or concern. Each group is to create a plan, based on the seven intelligences, for approaching the issue or concern. Students can decide to make posters, come up with slogans, write songs, create dance routines, conduct interviews with teachers and students, take personal opinion polls, and so on. Have each group share its plan and discuss possible next steps.

- **Toward Intelligence on TV.** Prerecord a slice of a soap opera, situation comedy, or detective show and show the recording to the class. At a critical turning point, stop the tape and, with your students, brainstorm seven possible intelligent decisions that the characters could make. Then start the video again and see what decisions the characters made and what happened as a result of the decisions. Discuss the pros and cons of the decisions made in the film as well as those you brainstormed.

- **Alternatives to World Problems.** As a whole class, study a contemporary global issue facing humanity. Divide students into seven small groups, one group for each intelligence. Have the groups think of alternatives, from the perspective of their assigned intelligence, that people should explore as a possible solution to the problem. Hold a mock United Nations meeting in which each group presents its recommendation.

- **Intelligent Approaches to Personal Problems.** Ask students to work alone and list three problems or issues with which they are struggling or challenges they are facing. Then have them select one problem from the list with which to work during this exercise. For the problem or issue they have selected, ask the students to list one possible approach for each intelligence. Now ask them to turn to a partner and share their approaches. The partners will suggest additional approaches that occur to them. The point of this activity is to find a variety of possible problem- or issue-solving approaches, not to analyze each other psychologically!

- **History or Literature Decisions Audit.** Place students in cooperative groups of three to four students. Ask them to use the seven intelligences to analyze key decisions that historical or literary figures made. Have the students discuss each decision based on questions similar to the following: "What was the governing intelligence behind this decision?" "What other decisions might have been made if other intelligences had been brought to bear on the decision?" "How might the outcomes have been different or similar had a multiple intelligence approach been used?"

- **Review Questions Variety Show.** Have students get into seven groups, each representing one of the seven ways of knowing. Have the students turn to the review questions at the end of a lesson or unit. Then have each group brainstorm intelligence-appropriate answers to the questions. Each group will create something in the modality of their assigned intelligence through which to share their answers with the rest of the class.

Problem Solving in 7 Steps
(Elementary)
Get seven ideas for each of the following suggestions.

What could you do to help if someone has . . .

An argument

Lost money

A sick friend

A broken window

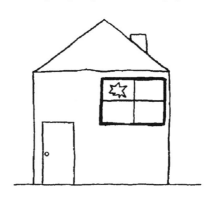

A broken toy

Been left out

Problem Solving in 7 Steps

(Middle School)

Choose three of the situations that follow and see if
you can think of seven "intelligent" responses for each!

What could you do if . . .

You have an argument with a good friend	You feel misunderstood by a parent
You lose something that is important to you	You are accused of something you didn't do
Someone double-crosses you	You get some bad news
You run out of allowance money before the end of a week	You can't find the homework that you did
A plan you made for something doesn't work	You get left out of an activity by your friends 

Problem Solving in 7 Steps

(Secondary)
Choose a partner, then together choose two
of the scenarios that follow and discuss them.

Can you solve these problems using the seven intelligences?

Scenario 1

Don, a high school junior, comes home from school to discover that his parents have grounded him for something he didn't do. In the past he has not always been totally honest with his parents, so there is a "trust gap" between them. Think of seven "intelligent" ways Don can approach this situation.

Scenario 2

Mary Jo, a high school senior, is planning on going into a business career. She has been rejected by her top three college choices, however, due to the low grades she made in several subjects during her last two years of high school. What are your seven "intelligent" suggestions about what she should do?

Scenario 3

Katrina has recently started to drive. The first time she is allowed to take the family car out by herself, she has a minor accident. She is struggling with how to tell her parents. What are seven "intelligent" ways she could break the news to them?

Scenario 4

Juan is a new student from Mexico. He is shy and doesn't speak English very well. Other students are making fun of him because he is different. See if you can come up with seven "intelligent" ways of helping other students understand and accept Juan.

Scenario 5

You have just discovered that one of your good friends has a serious, life-threatening disease. You want to reaffirm your friendship and your support. Make a list of at least seven "intelligent" ways you could communicate your support.

Scenario 6

Eric, a high school junior, comes from a classic disadvantaged family. For much of his schooling he has been in special education classes. He is considering going to college but is not sure he can make it. Think of seven "intelligent" ways you could encourage him to give it a try.

Seven Pathways of Learning © 1994 Zephyr Press, Tucson, Arizona

Teacher's Personal Reflection Log

PROBLEM SOLVING IN 7 STEPS

I have the following thoughts/insights about the Problem Solving in 7 Steps strategy:

I feel that the Problem Solving in 7 Steps strategy can help me in my teaching in the following ways:

As a learning process, the Problem Solving in 7 Steps strategy includes the following benefits for my students:

I have the following specific ideas for using the Problem Solving in 7 Steps strategy in my classroom in the near future:

I think the Problem Solving in 7 Steps strategy can be used beyond the classroom and school in the following ways:

Multiple Intelligence Roles in Cooperative Groups

INTRODUCTION

This lesson helps students learn how to use their multiple intelligences strategically to add excitement, depth, and breadth to a learning activity. Students will have an opportunity to play roles that embody the various intelligences to assist a cooperative learning group.

OBJECTIVE

The goal of the lesson is for students to learn the skill of playing different roles that will help a group succeed in its task.

DISCUSSION

This lesson is a multiple intelligence adaptation of one of the key strategies of cooperative learning: assigning students roles to play in groups. Multiple intelligences and cooperation go together like a hand and glove. Is it any surprise that cooperative group learning can provide a major boost to students' understanding of and willingness to use their seven ways of knowing? When students are allowed to play a role and everyone knows they are only playing a role, they often can transcend some of their inhibitions and weaknesses. When we actively and vividly imagine something to be real, the brain believes what we actively imagine. It does not know the difference. Think, for example, of what happens when you actively and vividly imagine your favorite food! In this lesson students have a chance to imagine that they are experts in performing various intelligence capacities or skills, the very capacities and skills that, when students are "just themselves," they may not be able to perform.

MULTIPLE INTELLIGENCE ROLES IN COOPERATIVE GROUPS

Lesson Procedures

1. Think of an upcoming lesson that lends itself nicely to a cooperative learning structure: a set of vocabulary words that students will need to learn, a reading assignment with distinct parts that individuals could study and teach to others, a set of math problems that students could help each other solve, and so on.

2. Have students get into teams of four. Carefully explain the academic task of the lesson (that is, what students are assigned to do, accomplish, and learn). Ask if there are any questions about the task.

3. After making the assignment and answering any questions, say, *"One of our concerns in this lesson is to make sure that we are using our multiple intelligences to help us with the learning goals. Therefore I am going to assign different intelligence roles to each of you so that you can help your group be as intelligent as possible during the lesson."* For possible roles you might assign, see the examples that follow this lesson (pp. 119–21).

   Students probably will not need to use seven roles in one lesson, so assign the four that you think are most appropriate. Students will need help in defining the "looks like" and "sounds like" behaviors associated with each role you have assigned. You will also need to decide if you are going to assign the roles randomly or if you will allow each group to make their own assignments.

4. Ask if there are any questions about the role assignments. If not, tell the groups they may go to work, but make sure that you monitor their work carefully, intervening as necessary to ensure that each group is successful.

5. When the time you have allotted for students to complete the assignment is up, have each team get together with another team and share

how they approached the lesson; that is, students will show their visual recordings, do their gesture or physical movements, and talk about what they did to encourage and support each other in the lesson.

6. After they have had time to share their work with the other groups, lead the whole class in the following discussion:

- *What was it like to use the different intelligences consciously to do this lesson?*
- *Which of the intelligence roles did your group like the most? Why?*
- *Which was most difficult? Why?*
- *What have you learned about how the different ways of knowing can enhance a lesson?*
- *How did this way of approaching a lesson help you?*
- *What things do you want to try again in future lessons?*

Multiple Intelligence Roles in Cooperative Groups Extensions

More Multiple Intelligence Roles in Cooperative Groups Lesson Ideas

The following are ideas you may adapt to your academic content.

- **Intelligent Figures from History.** Conduct a rapid brainstorming session in which students name figures from history that the students associate with each of the intelligences. Place the students in groups of seven. Assign students a contemporary issue to consider.

Each student chooses one historical figure from the list and pretends to be that person, discussing the contemporary issue from that person's point of view. Make sure all intelligences are represented in the figures students choose.

- **The "Remake" of Classical Stories.** As a class, choose a story or play you have been studying and discuss and analyze the work in terms of the different intelligences. Ask, "What is the dominant intelligence portrayed? Which intelligence is weak or almost absent? What new roles or characters would you add to bring about more of an intelligence balance? What changes in the plot might achieve this balance?" Have students get into groups of five; then have each group use the multiple intelligence factors to act out the story or play and see how the story changes.

- **"What's My (Intelligence) Line?"** Create multiple intelligence cards, each of which describes a role that might be helpful in a group situation. Have one student draw a role card out of a hat and study the description of the role for a moment. The rest of the class tries to guess the role by asking the student yes-or-no questions. A key to the success of this extension is to be outrageous, hilarious, and as creative as possible in naming and defining the roles.

- **Intelligence Roles Scenarios.** Create several problem scenarios that might occur in the typical school classroom, situations that could be improved by having students play various intelligence roles. Assign students to work in groups of five, and assign each group a different scenario to work on. The groups discuss the scenarios and decide what multiple intelligence roles are needed to solve the problem. The groups then create a dramatization of the situation that includes the new roles.

- **The MI Roles Catalogue.** With the whole class, brainstorm a list of all the possible roles you can think of that are related to the seven ways of knowing, from the sublime to the ridiculous. Have the students get into groups of three, then have them choose from the list one role for each intelligence and write five-point descriptions of the roles. As part of their report to the rest of the class have each group present a dramatic enactment of their favorite role.

- **"Different Strokes for Different Folks" (or Situations).** Have students get into groups of three or four to think about their lives beyond the classroom. Have them list situations in which they sometimes find themselves where playing certain multiple intelligence roles could help improve a difficult situation: a family disagreement, a club trying to make a difficult decision, peer relationships that seem to have stagnated, and so on.

Seven Pathways of Learning © 1994 Zephyr Press, Tucson, Arizona

Multiple Intelligence Roles in Cooperative Groups
(All Grades)

Verbal/Linguistic Roles

★ **Reader** is responsible for reading the written material that is necessary to complete a lesson the group is working on.

★ **Secretary** takes notes on the group's work and does any writing the lesson requires.

★ **Speller** checks all of the group's products for correct spelling.

★ **Reporter** communicates the results of the group's work to the rest of the class.

★ **Historian** keeps a record of key events that occur while the group is working.

★ **Poet** writes poems or limericks about the group and the work it has done in a lesson.

★ **Comedian** entertains the group with jokes, puns, and humorous comments about the lesson.

★ **Memory-jogger** helps the group create "remembering gimmicks" for a lesson.

★ **Debater** takes an opposing position in a discussion to promote thinking and discussion.

★ **Storyteller** tells others stories about the high and low points that occurred as the group worked on a task.

Logical/Mathematical Roles

★ **Checker** makes sure each group member understands the content and answers of the lesson.

★ **Scientist** helps the group create step-by-step procedures for an assigned task.

★ **Fortune-teller** makes predictions about the outcome of the group's work.

★ **Numbers expert** checks any math the group performs and the numbers it uses.

★ **Problem solver** suggests different ways to deal with a problem the group is to solve.

★ **Detective** looks for answer clues as the group works on solving the problem.

★ **Timekeeper** watches the clock during timed tasks and adjusts the pace as needed.

★ **Calculator** performs math operations for the group.

★ **Thinker** helps the group remember, evaluate, and improve its thinking steps.

★ **Patterns expert** looks for connections to other subject areas, both in and beyond the classroom.

Visual/Spatial Roles

★ **Architect** helps the group create a "blueprint" or master plan for the final product.

★ **Colorizer** suggests color ideas to express the group's feelings and ideas in the final product.

★ **Drawer** produces images or pictures to illustrate different parts of an assigned lesson.

★ **Visualizer** helps the group think in images and pictures using the "eyes of the mind."

★ **Shapes expert** makes any abstract design and patterns to go along with the team's work.

★ **Locator** makes sure the group is at the right place on a page or can find its way on a map.

★ **Sculptor** helps the group express its ideas and feelings through manipulatives, such as clay.

★ **Cutter** does any paper cutting or tearing the group needs done.

★ **Symbolizer** creates symbols and images of the group's identity or any key ideas.

★ **Dreamer** helps the group use its active imagination to understand a lesson more fully.

Multiple Intelligence Roles in Cooperative Groups
(All Grades)

Bodily/Kinesthetic Roles

★ **Actor** helps the group think of role-playing ideas for acting out parts of a lesson.

★ **Dancer** suggests creative physical movements that could be part of the group's report.

★ **Coach** helps a group learn physical movement routines to embody what the group learns.

★ **Inventor** creates new steps, procedures, and active ways to do old things.

★ **Choreographer** helps the group plan its staging of a report or presentation.

★ **Gesture manager** suggests body language to communicate group feelings about a lesson.

★ **Athletic coordinator** thinks of physical games to play that are related to a lesson or task.

★ **Mimer** creates nonverbal ways to show what the group has learned in a lesson or activity.

★ **Stage director** helps the group practice and perfect an upcoming presentation.

★ **Props manager** helps the group find any presentation props it needs.

Musical/Rhythmic Roles

★ **Drummer** makes up rhythmic patterns to match the "beat" of the stages of the group's work.

★ **Singer** thinks of popular songs or tunes about the group and the specific task it is doing.

★ **Sound director** helps the group plan appropriate background sounds for a report.

★ **Composer** makes up words for songs about the group and the assignment it is doing.

★ **Volume controller** ensures the group's noise does not rise above an appropriate level during a cooperative task.

★ **Music coach** rehearses the group in the musical parts of a report that is to be presented.

★ **Rapper** helps the group create raps and jingles about itself and its work.

★ **Rhythm coordinator** cues the group when it is to perform various rhythmic patterns.

★ **Choral director** leads the group in any musical or rap parts of a presentation or report.

★ **Instrument manager** gathers or creates the noise and sound makers the group needs.

Seven Pathways of Learning © 1994 Zephyr Press, Tucson, Arizona

Multiple Intelligence Roles in Cooperative Groups
(All Grades)

Intrapersonal Roles

★ **Worrier** is concerned about whether the group is doing what it is supposed to be doing.

★ **Reflector** helps the group think about the significance and implications of a task.

★ **Processor** leads the group in evaluating its thinking and cooperative behavior.

★ **Quality controller** ensures that the group is doing its best possible work and that the final product is good.

★ **Creativity manager** helps the group think of unique and fun approaches to an assigned task.

★ **Feelings watcher** pays attention to and helps the group discuss its affective responses to a task.

★ **Learning-awareness catalyzer** helps the group be conscious about what it is learning.

★ **Connection maker** helps the group see links with other subjects, both in and beyond the classroom.

★ **Concentration technologist** suggests ways the group can maintain its focus on an assignment.

★ **Philosopher** raises questions about values and beliefs that emerge as the group works.

Interpersonal Roles

★ **Organizer** helps the group plan and agree on strategies for approaching an assigned task.

★ **Encourager** provides positive support and encouragement for the members of the group.

★ **Motivator** finds ways to keep each group member excited about an assignment.

★ **Counselor** advises the group on how to deal with any problems or issues that may arise.

★ **Interpreter** explains the meaning of any parts of the group's work that others don't understand.

★ **Involvement manager** ensures that each group member contributes to the final product.

★ **Task master** helps the group stay on task and makes sure all parts of a task are completed.

★ **Consensus maker** makes sure that all members agree on and understand the final product.

★ **Communications watcher** guards the group's interaction processes (listening, hearing, and so on).

★ **Paraphraser** repeats what various members of the group are saying to help all understand.

Teacher's Personal Reflection Log

MULTIPLE INTELLIGENCE ROLES IN COOPERATIVE GROUPS

I have the following thoughts/insights about the Multiple Roles in Cooperative Groups strategy:

I feel that the Multiple Roles in Cooperative Groups strategy can help me in my teaching in the following ways:

As a learning process, the Multiple Roles in Cooperative Groups strategy includes the following benefits for my students:

I have the following specific ideas for using the Multiple Roles in Cooperative Groups strategy in my classroom in the near future:

I think the Multiple Roles in Cooperative Groups strategy can be used beyond the classroom and school in the following ways:

Seven Pathways of Learning © 1994 Zephyr Press, Tucson, Arizona

EXPLORING INTELLIGENCE CAPACITIES WITH A PARTNER

Lesson Procedures

1. Have students get into groups of two or three using grouping criteria that provide maximum heterogeneity.

2. On the overhead or board display the appropriate work sheet from pages 126–128. Say, *"Each group will randomly select one of these items and plan a presentation for the rest of the class."* Following are several random selection methods each group can use to choose an item from the work sheet:

   - Use the sixth digit in the telephone number of the tallest person in the group.
   - Each member puts one hand behind his or her back, holds up a number of fingers, and then brings the hand out; add the numbers.
   - Each person rolls a number on some dice; the group adds up its members' numbers, then divides the sum by the number of members in the group.
   - The group takes the average of their shoe sizes.
   - Use the number of people in the family of the group member with the largest family.
   - Use the number of letters in the name of the person with the curliest hair.

3. Give the groups ten to fifteen minutes to work out their presentations. Carefully monitor the groups as they work, intervening as necessary to ensure that each group succeeds at its assigned task.

4. When the groups have completed their assignments, have each group make its presentation to the whole class.

5. Lead the whole class in the following discussion about the lesson:

   - *What do you remember from these presentations? (This is a group "remembering" reflection.)*

Exploring Intelligence Capacities with a Partner

INTRODUCTION

In this lesson students have an opportunity to learn how to "translate" various verbal/linguistic or logical/mathematical lesson content into the unique "language" or modality of the different intelligences. Most of the material we have to teach is pre-packaged in a verbal/linguistic or logical/mathematical form. This lesson helps students go beyond these constraints.

OBJECTIVE

The goal of the lesson is to teach students how to reconceptualize a task in terms of all seven ways of knowing and how to see the multiple ways in which students can approach their schoolwork.

DISCUSSION

One of the presuppositions of this lesson is that students often learn better, more willingly, and more quickly from their peers than from an outside authority figure. The lesson capitalizes on this phenomenon by asking students to figure out with a partner how to perform certain tasks. This approach not only provides the needed peer support, but also allows students to build new levels of trust and a willingness to risk. The key to success in the lesson is for students to know that there is no right answer or right way of performing the skills they select. What you are after is having them stretch themselves beyond their usual and comfortable ways of operating. Make sure that the list of tasks is slightly outrageous and fun.

- *What were your feelings as you worked with your group?*
- *What were your feelings as you made your   presentation to the class?*
- *What were your feelings as you watched the   different presentations?*
- *What ideas do you have about how we could incorporate what we have done in this intelligence lesson into our daily classroom work?*

Exploring Intelligence Capacities with a Partner Extensions

More Exploring Intelligence Capacities with a Partner Lesson Ideas

The following are ideas you may adapt to your academic content.

- **Subject Area Theater.** List the basic skills that students need to be able to perform as part of a given subject area. Have students work with partners and choose a skill from the list, using the same random selection processes outlined in the lesson. Then have the pairs create a demonstration from everyday life that shows the skills they have chosen.

- **Stop the Action and Respond.** Have one student start telling a well-known story, historical event, or math or science process to another. At a certain point in the narration, ring a bell and inject some new and unexpected element or information that requires the performance of some multiple intelligence skill (for example,

Goldilocks is deaf and so the bears can only draw pictures, or multiplication has suddenly been destroyed). The story-teller's partner must perform the required skill, then tell what happens next. You may choose to ring the bell and switch between the partners several times during the activity.

- **Illustrating a Lecture with MI Stuff.** Put an outline of a lecture that is central to the day's lesson on the overhead or board. Start going through the lecture, pausing at certain points and asking students to do MI activities related to what you've been presenting; they might think of a piece of music they would play, a physical movement they would perform, a visual image they would draw, and so on.

- **Intelligence Workout Routines.** For certain rote learning or memorization tasks in a given subject area, help students devise mnemonic devices, based on the seven intelligences, to help them remember the information: rap times tables, visual symbols for the parts of speech, body gestures for science concepts, and so on. Then have students create an exercise routine to use to practice the information.

- **Intelligence Roulette Review.** Have each student find a partner. Before the lesson, turn the Capacities Inventory Wheel (p. 21) into a roulette wheel or a wheel with a spinner. Ask the class review questions for a unit you have just completed. After asking each question, spin the wheel. The capacity on which the wheel stops is the one the partners must use to answer the question. Give the students time to work together; then call on different pairs to give their response using the capacity that came up on the wheel.

- **Subject Area Trivia.** Design a trivia game based on specific content of subject areas you want students to know, maybe as a review for an upcoming examination. The trivia you ask students should include all seven intelligences: the dance that was made famous in Vienna (they must name the waltz and show how to do it), the design of a nautilus shell (they must be able to draw it), and so on.

Exploring Intelligence Capacities with a Partner
(Elementary)

Tell the story of the "Three Little Pigs" in a song.	**Spell your name with your body.**
Listen to a story and tell it to someone else.	**Make numbers into people and animals.**
Have a conversation with a rock.	**Tell a partner some of the questions you have about life.**
Look at a picture and tell a story about it.	**Make up a number pattern to stump a friend.**

Exploring Intelligence Capacities with a Partner
(Middle School)

Tell a story you've read recently through song, rap, and music.	**Read something, making different sounds for the punctuation marks.**
Draw pictures to show what goes on in adding, subtracting, multiplying, and dividing.	**Concentrate on an object and record your feelings and thoughts about it.**
Tell a story about a picture. What do you think is happening?	**Draw a picture of an experience while a partner tells you about it.**
Make up body movements or gestures to match a piece of music.	**Create a secret code for the alphabet; then write a message using the code.**
Tell a partner how to do something; then watch her or him do it!	**Make up a drama about something you've studied in science.**

Exploring Intelligence Capacities with a Partner
(Secondary)

Create a "Shakespeare Rap" to tell the story of a play.	**Make up an outline for a television soap opera based on a scientific process.**
Write a story in which the characters are mathematical operations, symbols, or processes.	**Listen to a piece of music and draw any shapes, designs, images, and pictures it evokes in you.**
Pretend you can have a conversation with a historical or literary figure. What advice would you seek? How would this person answer your questions?	**Draw a picture or diagram (with color!) of how to find the hypotenuse of a right triangle, the "x" factor in an equation, or a square root.**
"Illustrate" a piece of poetry with appropriate background sounds, rhythms, tones, and other noises.	**Make a logical outline that explains the emotional flow and impact of a piece of music.**
Make up a series of gestures or physical movements to embody key concepts or ideas you have been studying.	**Create a skit to show a scientific process, a math formula, or the classical structure of a persuasive speech.**
Write a description of your opinion of a piece of art—what you like, don't like, what it "says" to you, and so on.	**Listen to a partner tell you how she or he solved a problem; then explain the process to others.**
Make a list of "life questions" raised by a piece of poetry or other literature.	**Imagine the digestive system, the respiratory system, the circulatory system, and the brain having a conversation about a current events topic. Record what each might say.**

Seven Pathways of Learning © 1994 Zephyr Press, Tucson, Arizona

Teacher's Personal Reflection Log

EXPLORING INTELLIGENCE CAPACITIES WITH A PARTNER

I have the following thoughts/insights about the Exploring Intelligence Capacities with a Partner strategy:

I feel that the Exploring Intelligence Capacities with a Partner strategy can help me in my teaching in the following ways:

As a learning process, the Exploring Intelligence Capacities with a Partner strategy includes the following benefits for my students:

I have the following specific ideas for using the Exploring Intelligence Capacities with a Partner strategy in my classroom in the near future:

I think the Exploring Intelligence Capacities with a Partner strategy can be used beyond the classroom and school in the following ways:

Intelligence Triggers

INTRODUCTION

This lesson gives students an opportunity to state what helps them turn on the different intelligences. While we all have all seven ways of knowing, certain gimmicks or techniques may give us access to certain intelligences more quickly and effectively than other techniques.

OBJECTIVE

The goal of the lesson is to make students aware of the methods, tools, and techniques students use to gain quick access to each intelligence, and to allow them to name their favorite methods.

DISCUSSION

One of the key research findings related to the theory of multiple intelligences is that, given the intelligences' basis in the neurological system, they are easily triggered or awakened through certain external and internal stimuli. The key to using this information effectively to enhance one's use of multiple intelligences in everyday life is knowing what these awakening triggers are. In my first book, *Seven Ways of Knowing,* I present numerous exercises, games, puzzles, and practices for achieving this awakening. This lesson is designed to create a strategic awareness of what is involved in accessing the various intelligence modalities. It is also important to recognize, however, that every awakening exercise or technique does not work equally well for each person, given the diversity of our sociocultural backgrounds.

INTELLIGENCE TRIGGERS
Lesson Procedures

1. Pass out a marking pen and seven 3"-by-5" self-stick notes, one for each intelligence, to each student.
2. Project the seven intelligences Toolbox (pp. 133–34) on the overhead or post the chart on the board. Say, *"In this lesson we are going to create a Multiple Intelligence Toolbox to help us use all of our intelligences in our classroom. We will start by brainstorming a list of favorite tools and activities for each intelligence."*

   Note: refer to Multiple Intelligence Toolbox to help students think of additional tools

3. Go through the intelligences one by one, asking students to write their favorite tool for accessing each intelligence, one tool for one intelligence per self-stick note.
4. Divide the board or a wall in the classroom into seven sections, one for each intelligence. Give students a couple of minutes to stick their self-stick notes in the appropriate sections.
5. As a whole class, look at the tools listed, clustering any that are the same. After organizing the tools, make a couple of summary statements regarding what the organization tells you: "It looks like a lot of us really like to draw," or "There doesn't seem to be a favorite for this one—look at the variety of tools we like."
6. Have students form groups of two or three with their neighbors. The groups' first task is to understand the tools suggested for triggering each intelligence and add any other tools they think of as a team. Be on hand to answer questions as they arise.
7. When students have completed their discussion of the tools, pass out the work sheet on page 135 to each student. Have students individually choose two tools for each intelligence that they like and that work best for them, and write them on the work sheet by the pluses under the appropriate intelligence. Then have them list by

the minuses on the work sheet one tool for each intelligence that may work for someone else but does nothing for them.

8. Have students concentrate on one intelligence at a time and share with their groups the tools they listed on the work sheets. Make sure each student explains why she or he marked certain tools.

   Note: The information on the work sheets can help you plan future lessons, so you may want to have students sign the toolboxes and to collect the signed toolboxes. You can then include in your lessons multiple intelligence teaching strategies that take into account the things your students like, and you can determine those tools your students need help to use effectively.

9. Lead the class in the following implications reflection:

   - *What did you find interesting about creating the toolbox? What was exciting? Surprising? Confusing? Helpful?*
   - *If you were going to explain our toolbox to someone who wasn't here today, such as one of your parents, a younger brother or sister, or one of your grandparents, what would you tell that person the toolbox is?*
   - *In what ways do you think the toolbox can help you with your daily classroom work? How can it help you with your homework?*

   Note: You may want to leave the list of the brainstormed tools up as a permanent reference.

Intelligence Trigger Extensions

More Intelligence Trigger Lesson Ideas

The following are ideas you may adapt to your academic content.

- **Awakening Intelligence in Others.** Place students into groups of three or four. Give each group an outline of the lessons you have planned for a week and the particular intelligence you have decided to emphasize in each lesson. Assign each group a lesson. The groups are to create the awakening stage for their assigned lesson. (See Lazear 1991b for a description of the awakening stage of multiple intelligence lessons.) This stage is similar to Madeline Hunter's "anticipatory set" but focuses more on anticipating the intelligence that will be emphasized in a lesson by preparing the brain to work in the language, jargon, symbol system, and mode of a given intelligence. Each group will then lead the class in triggering the intelligence that will be emphasized in the assigned lesson.

- **Triggering Your Own Intelligence.** Introduce students to a lesson by telling them your objective for the lesson and the particular intelligence that you will be emphasizing. Allow students a few

Seven Pathways of Learning © 1994 Zephyr Press, Tucson, Arizona

minutes to prepare to use the targeted intelligence by using whatever trigger works best for them. A list of suggested triggers will give students some options from which to choose until students are more confident and knowledgeable about what is involved in awakening the different intelligences.

- **What Got Triggered for You?** Show students a video or film that is full of various intelligence capacities or skills: a great soundtrack, juicy dialogue, plenty of action, glorious visual effects, and so on. During the movie ask students to be aware of what intelligences are being stimulated in themselves. Afterward, discuss what happened and how the filmmakers made it happen: What triggering techniques did the film makers use? Also ask students how they knew a particular intelligence had been triggered.

- **Intelligence Report Options.** Assign students a research report about specific information or content you want them to investigate as part of a particular unit of study. They are to use at least two intelligences besides verbal/linguistic intelligence. Pair students with partners and ask the pairs to discuss the various options, getting ideas from each other. Have each student turn in a written description of his or her research or report plan. Once you have read the plans, you may need to have a special meeting with some students to ensure their success.

- **Intelligence Triggers in Everyday Life.** On the overhead projector or blackboard, display a time line of a day, starting with getting up, then moving on to getting ready, eating breakfast, traveling to school, and so on. Place students in groups of three to four and ask them to list "natural" intelligence triggers that are more or less a given part of each section of the time line: sounds, images, conversation with others, physical movement, and so on. Have students list ideas for helping themselves be more aware of these things.

- **Test Options/Alternatives.** Have students work together to prepare for an upcoming examination. Encourage them to use any of the intelligences or combinations of intelligences to make sure they are on top of the information you will be testing for. Also ask them to give you input for creating an intelligence-fair test that would let them use different intelligences to demonstrate mastery of material.

Teacher's Reference
Multiple Intelligence Toolbox[4]
(Elementary)

TOOLS TO HELP YOU BE SMART!

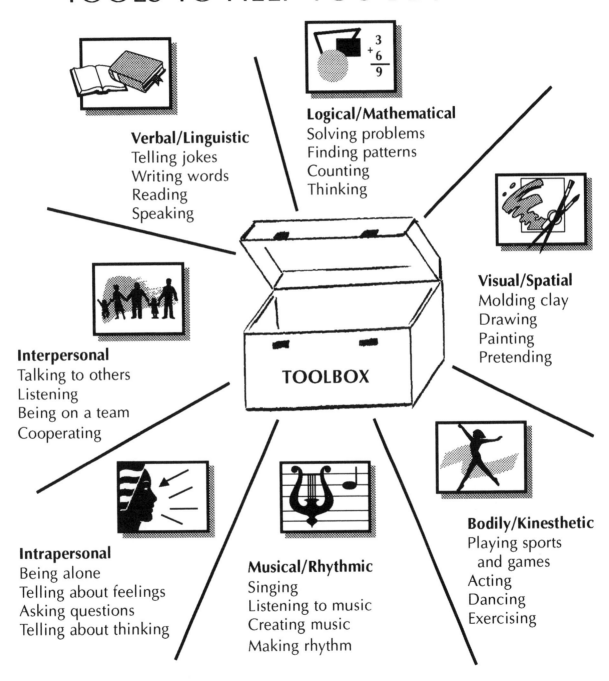

Verbal/Linguistic
Telling jokes
Writing words
Reading
Speaking

Logical/Mathematical
Solving problems
Finding patterns
Counting
Thinking

Visual/Spatial
Molding clay
Drawing
Painting
Pretending

Interpersonal
Talking to others
Listening
Being on a team
Cooperating

TOOLBOX

Bodily/Kinesthetic
Playing sports
 and games
Acting
Dancing
Exercising

Intrapersonal
Being alone
Telling about feelings
Asking questions
Telling about thinking

Musical/Rhythmic
Singing
Listening to music
Creating music
Making rhythm

4. Adaped from Lazear, David. *Seven Ways of Knowing.* Palatine, Ill.: Skylight, 1991.

Teacher's Reference
Multiple Intelligence Toolbox[5]
(Middle School & Secondary)

Verbal/Linguistic
- Reading
- Vocabulary
- Formal speech
- Journal or diary keeping
- Creative writing
- Poetry
- Oral debate
- Impromptu speaking
- Humor or telling jokes
- Storytelling

Logical/Mathematical
- Abstract symbols and formulas
- Outlining
- Graphic organizers
- Number sequences
- Calculation
- Deciphering codes
- Forcing relationships
- Syllogisms
- Problem solving
- Pattern games

Bodily/Kinesthetic
- Folk or creative dance
- Role-playing
- Physical gestures
- Drama
- Martial arts
- Body language
- Physical exercise
- Mime
- Inventing
- Sports

Visual/Spatial
- Guided imagery
- Active imagination
- Color schemes
- Patterns and designs
- Painting
- Drawing
- Mind mapping
- Pretending
- Sculpture
- Pictures

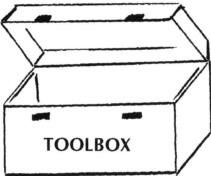

TOOLBOX

Interpersonal
- Giving feedback
- Intuiting others' feelings
- Cooperative learning strategies
- Person-to-person communication
- Empathy practices
- Division of labor
- Collaboration skills
- Receiving feedback
- Sensing others' motives
- Group projects

Intrapersonal
- Silent reflection methods
- Metacognition techniques
- Thinking strategies
- Emotional processing
- "Know thyself" practices
- Mindfulness practices
- Focusing and concentration skills
- Higher-order reasoning
- Complex guided imagery
- "Centering" practices

Musical/Rhythmic
- Rhythmic patterns
- Vocal sounds and tones
- Music composition and creation
- Percussion vibrations
- Humming
- Environmental sounds
- Instrumental sounds
- Singing
- Tonal patterns
- Music performance

5. Adapted from Lazear, David. *Seven Ways of Knowing*. Palatine, Ill.: Skylight, 1991.

Intelligence Triggers
(All Grades)

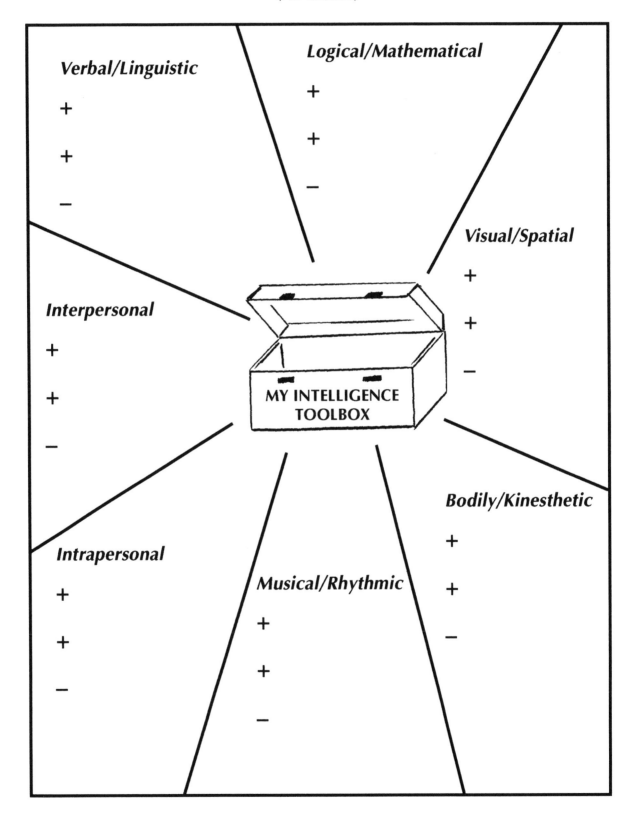

Teacher's Personal Reflection Log
INTELLIGENCE TRIGGERS

I have the following thoughts/insights about the Intelligence Triggers strategy:

I feel that the Intelligence Triggers strategy can help me in my teaching in the following ways:

As a learning process, the Intelligence Triggers strategy includes the following benefits for my students:

I have the following specific ideas for using the Intelligence Triggers strategy in my classroom in the near future:

I think the Intelligence Triggers strategy can be used beyond the classroom and school in the following ways:

Seven Pathways of Learning © 1994 Zephyr Press, Tucson, Arizona

INTELLIGENCE COACHING

Lesson Procedures

1. Assign the class to work with partners. Try to pair each student with a partner who has different intelligence strengths and weaknesses from her or his own.
2. Tell students their task is to coach each other on how to use the seven ways of knowing to improve their performance in school. On the overhead or board, show students the coaching model or process that is appropriate for their grade level (see pp. 140–42).
3. Explain the coaching process as follows:

> *For the next month (or longer, if students seem ready and willing), we are going to experiment with being intelligence coaches for each other. At the end of each week you will meet with your coach and review the week. You will share with your partner homework you have done and tests you have taken, and you will talk generally about how the week has gone. As you share, you are to discover the areas in which your partner had difficulty and discuss how your partner might have employed different intelligences to help. In light of this conversation, you will help your partner think of ways she or he can use the intelligences in the coming week. When your coaching session is over, each of you will have an intelligence action plan for improving your performance during the next week.*

You may need to point out that it is okay for students to get together to coach each other at times other than those you set aside, but that once a week they will have time in class to coach each other.

4. Discuss any issues you feel will clarify the process and its intent and answer any questions students have.
5. Give students a chance to practice the coaching process using a relatively simple situation. Your goal in this step is to allow students to

Intelligence Coaching

INTRODUCTION

This lesson teaches students how they can help and encourage each other to use the full spectrum of their intellectual capacities, both in school and beyond the classroom.

OBJECTIVE

The goal of the lesson is to teach students the basic steps of the coaching model and to have students practice using the model to be more successful in school.

DISCUSSION

Learning to coach others in the intelligences is probably the most advanced process presented in this book. Coaching requires not only a great deal of sensitivity to other people, but also an in-depth knowledge of the intelligences. Nonetheless, students are fully capable of coaching each other in the manner described in the lesson if they are taught how to do it, are given time to practice, and are given time at least once a week to work on their coaching relationships.

learn the process so they feel comfortable with the process and with relating to each other in this way. Later, they will transfer the coaching process to academic situations. See the examples for possible practice scenarios.

6. Give the pairs time to try the coaching model and to get to know each other in this new way.

7. At the end of the allotted time, have the partners thank each other for the help each has given. Ask students to talk about what happened, sharing the positive and negative aspects of being each other's coaches:

- *What was the best part of being a coach for your partner? What was the worst part?*
- *Did you like coaching? Why or why not?*
- *Are you willing to try coaching for a month and see how you feel then?*
- *What questions did this exercise raise for you? What parts of the process don't you understand?*
- *In what ways do you think this kind of coaching might help you?*

Note: These questions might also be used after the weekly coaching session to get students' feedback on how it is going.

Intelligence Coaching Extensions

More Intelligence Coaching Lesson Ideas

The following are ideas you may adapt to your academic content.

- **Homework Preparation Coaching.** After giving a homework assignment, especially one that is difficult or one that deals with new concepts, give students time to work in their coaching teams to help each other understand the assignment and to discuss the best way to approach it. Remember, not everyone will approach the assignment in the same way, but the coaching task is to help each partner find his or her best way.

- **Intelligence Test Preparation.** Have students work with their coaches to prepare for an upcoming test. Each member of the coaching team tells the other how to prepare for the test using the seven ways of knowing. The partners then work with each other to review, using the intelligence strategy or strategies discussed earlier. You must be on hand to assist the teams in this exercise.

- **Unit Reviews.** When you are finishing a unit of study, have students pair up in their coaching teams to discuss, review, and pull the unit together. The teams are to create a way to summarize the unit in such a way that they not only review the individual parts of the unit but also understand the "big picture" of the unit, seeing how all the parts relate to one another. The coaching teams are to choose an intelligence as the medium for the review and then produce their summary. Remember, you may get everything from murals, to songs, to mind maps, to outlines, to dances. The key point is that students have grasped the knowledge in the unit.

- **What Went Wrong?** After you have corrected a test or a homework assignment, have students work with their coaches to understand and correct mistakes the students made. Encourage students to discuss how they used the different ways of knowing to help them with the assignment or test and to think of intelligent things they could do next time to improve their performance. If students desire, allow them to retake the test or redo the homework.

- **Planning for Peak Performance.** Ask students each to list two or three upcoming situations in which they feel they will need to be performing at their absolute best: an oral report, a sports event, a music recital, a final exam, and so on. Have students share their lists in their coaching teams. Then give them time to help their partners create a winning plan so they are ready to realize their potential in the situations listed. Students' suggestions for each other might include mental rehearsal, verbal affirmations, trial runs, visual diagrams of the steps involved, and so on.

- **Evaluating Problem-Solving Strategies.** Have students individually write down the steps they usually go through when they are trying to solve problems. Have coaching partners compare their problem-solving steps and discuss the positive and negative aspects of each, including how well the step works. Finally, have coaching pairs work together to create a new approach that incorporates the best steps from the two approaches. Students will discuss problems they have had in the past and how they think the new approach would have helped.

Intelligence Coaching
(Elementary)

HELPING EACH OTHER

Coaching Steps

1. **SHARE your work**
2. **TELL about hard times**
3. **SHARE ideas to help**
4. **PLAN next steps**

Find Seven Ways to . . .

Meet new friends	**Tell a good story**
Make a hard decision	**Learn to use good manners**
Learn spelling words	**Teach counting to 25**

Intelligence Coaching
(Middle)

COACHING YOUR PARTNER

Coaching Steps

1. **SHARE basic information**
2. **DISCUSS your feelings**
3. **Track PAST intelligence**
4. **Think of new INTELLIGENCE strategies to help**
5. **PLAN for next week**

Practice Scenarios

1. **Talk about a difficult decision you made in the last year.** *How could the seven ways of knowing have helped you?*

2. **Pretend you can replay a past family problem.** *Think of ways the seven intelligences could have been used.*

3. **Share some homework or a test that you "bombed."** *What new intelligence strategies would you use if you could redo the homework or retake the test?*

4. **Talk about an argument with a friend.** *How can you use the seven intelligences to work things out?*

5. **Discuss some things you really want to buy.** *Think of at least seven money-raising ideas—one for each of the intelligences.*

6. **Discuss saying "NO!" to drugs.** *How could you use the language of each intelligence to say "NO!"*

Intelligence Coaching
(Secondary)

COACHING MODEL

Coaching Steps

1. **Share basic information**

2. **Intelligence analysis/processing (Feelings)**

3. **Intelligence strategy plotting (Past)**

4. **Intelligence strategy plotting (Future)**

5. **Intelligence action planning (Performance)**

Practice Scenarios

1. **Discuss a family situation with which you feel you could use some help. Help each other understand the situation and think of alternatives.**

2. **Think through a problem your school is facing. With your partner, explore all the options you can think of for solving it.**

3. **Coach each other on a recent school assignment that was difficult or on which you received a low grade. What could you have done to do better on the assignment?**

4. **Discuss multiple approaches to a peer relations issue you are facing. *Note:* Stay focused on your own, not another's, problem.**

5. **Give each other advice and think of ideas about using the seven intelligences to resist the temptation to do drugs, including alcohol.**

6. **Think together about dealing creatively with challenges you'll face when you finish high school (for example, career directions, college, a job, marriage, and so on).**

Seven Pathways of Learning © 1994 Zephyr Press, Tucson, Arizona

Teacher's Personal Reflection Log

INTELLIGENCE COACHING

I have the following thoughts/insights about the Intelligence Coaching strategy:

I feel that the Intelligence Coaching strategy can help me in my teaching in the following ways:

As a learning process, the Intelligence Coaching strategy includes the following benefits for my students:

I have the following specific ideas for using the Intelligence Coaching strategy in my classroom in the near future:

I think the Intelligence Coaching strategy can be used beyond the classroom and school in the following ways:

NOTES TO PARENTS

The Strategic Level of the Seven Ways of Knowing

When we move to working at the strategic level of learning about the seven ways of knowing, we move to the conscious use of the different intelligences to help us solve problems and meet the challenges of daily living. My concern is to help students become aware of the vast kitbag of intelligence tools, techniques, and methods they have at their disposal as close as in their own brains. Part of being able to use the different ways of knowing strategically, however, involves learning how to make an intelligence work in a given situation, which involves learning to trust and interpret the intelligences when we are doing actual tasks that involve knowing, learning, and understanding.

The strategic level involves helping children develop knowledge about the intelligences, including what different capacities or skills are involved, how to trigger the intelligences in the brain, and how to strengthen and enhance the intelligences. This knowledge will give students enough confidence to employ the different ways of knowing on a regular basis to deepen learning, expand creativity, and improve problem-solving abilities. This is the ability to use the intelligences with intention.

Part of the task is to teach children who are working at this level how to use each of the intelligences to gain knowledge and to achieve certain learning objectives. As parents who care about our children's success in school, we may be most concerned with our children's ability at this level. We parents must reeducate ourselves concerning what school is all about. Our culture has told us that school is about educating our children in the "three Rs." I agree with this statement. I also believe, however, that school is about much more. A child can learn the three Rs and still not be equipped to live in his or her time. As I have mentored my own daughters through their schooling, I must confess that I have been far more excited by those classes and teachers who focused on timeless methods for living than by those who were preoccupied by the content of a particular subject. In our society's current situation, which has been described by some as a "knowledge explosion," more than 80 percent of the content we require our children to learn today will have significantly changed by the time they graduate. Teaching children how to learn seems to me to be the more important task, for when the content does change, our children will know how to learn the new content. It's a bit like the old Chinese proverb: Which is better, giving someone a fish, which will feed him or her for a day, or teaching someone how to fish, which will feed the person for a lifetime? I want my daughters and all children to be educated for a lifetime!

Seven Pathways of Learning © 1994 Zephyr Press, Tucson, Arizona

We must use the current content, which is the best we've got, to teach our children how to be as intelligent, on as many levels, using as many different approaches as they and we can find. Yes, our children must master certain content areas, and they must be able to produce on the various examinations our culture deems important. But *how* they master this assigned material must be given weight equal with the material itself.

Am I suggesting that the three Rs are no longer important? Far from it. Current statistics show clearly, however, that our present educational system and teaching methods are less than successful at teaching students the Three Rs, even though those subjects are currently our primary goal. As a father, I am excited about and committed to the theory of multiple intelligences because, when this way of teaching and learning is actively employed in the classroom, more of our children can and will succeed in school more of the time.

Following are some suggestions for nurturing the strategic development of all seven ways of knowing in your children. All of these suggestions assume that you are actively involved in your children's schooling and learning. Try some of these suggestions and see what happens. Encourage your children's teachers to learn about and use multiple intelligences in their teaching. Yes, miracles are still possible!

Activities to Support the Strategic Use of the Intelligences

Verbal/Linguistic

★ Experiment with nontraditional ways to study English: learning the parts of speech or punctuation through drawing, physical actions, and music.

★ When your child has written an essay or report, take the opposite side from the one she took and ask her to defend what she has written.

★ Encourage your child to "think on his feet" by asking him unexpected questions about things he has been studying.

★ Ask your child to create a sequel to a history lesson ("What would have happened if . . . ") or to turn a historical event into a modern story.

★ Help your child use a story grid (see p. 148 for examples) to brainstorm ideas for any writing assignment.

Logical/Mathematical

★ Create a list of good homework practices and have your child evaluate herself when she has completed assignments.

★ Once your child has completed an assignment, have him do something creative and fun using what he has learned.

★ Devise ways for your child to use what she is studying at home: dividing a pizza so each family member gets two pieces, integrating vocabulary words into the dinner conversation, and so on.

★ Help your child use graphic organizers (see chapter 4) to analyze and understand what he is studying: a character-attribute web, a comparison/contrast Venn diagram for math processes, a classification matrix for parts of speech, and so on.

Visual/Spatial

★ Help your child prepare for a test by drawing pictures of the concepts and visually mapping relationships between concepts she is studying.

★ Ask your child to draw a symbol or image to go along with his homework or what he has been studying.

★ Help your child visualize alternative solutions to story problems she is trying to solve in math.

★ Have your child enter an imaginary conversation with some person, thing, or concept, in a lesson.

★ Lead your child in "pretend you are there" imagination exercises to learn concepts in history, social studies, or literature lessons.

Bodily/Kinesthetic

★ Have your child use physical action and movement to embody the meanings of foreign language vocabulary words.

★ Have your child role-play key concepts she must learn: the three branches of our government or the Bill of Rights, for example.

★ When your child is studying another culture in social studies, have him help prepare food from the culture, dress in costumes from it, and create decor typical of that culture for your house.

★ To help your child understand math concepts and operations such as working with fractions, have her physically subtract two family members from the group, or divide the family into halves, then into thirds.

Activities to Support the Strategic Use of the Intelligences

Musical/Rhythmic

★ Have your child experiment with playing different kinds of background music while doing homework for different subject areas.

★ Help your child create raps or songs, such as the "ABC song," to memorize various facts: states and capitals, the major food groups, multiplication times tables, classifications of living things, and so on.

★ When your child is studying a period in history or another culture, play music from that period or culture and help her learn to sing some of the folk songs from that culture.

★ Work with your child to help him use sound to illustrate things he is studying: the sound of different punctuation marks (a la Victor Borge's "phonetic punctuation"), the sound of math operations (for example, +, =, >, ÷, ×), the sounds that should accompany a story, and so on.

Interpersonal

★ Divide a homework assignment into sections, and have each family member learn one part and teach it to the others; give a quiz to make sure each member "got it."

★ For a research project in any subject, help your child map out a research plan, including frequent reports to the family about what she is learning; then help her create a multimodal report for the class.

★ Create a game in which the whole family helps a child prepare for a test: "Mammals Trivia," "Parts-of-Speech Bingo," "Math-Operations Jeopardy," "Dates-in-History Wheel of Fortune," and so on.

★ When your child has a paper to write, ask the family to brainstorm ideas for the paper; the child will write the paper using whatever ideas seem appropriate, and the rest of the family will give feedback and ask questions.

Intrapersonal

★ Buy your child a special notebook in which to track his thinking and learning; he might use it to write about the main idea of a lesson, or to tell what he finds interesting or boring about a lesson, and so on.

★ Have your child pretend she can become what she is studying in science and learn about it from the "inside out"; she might become a plant to learn about photosynthesis, imagine being an insect and tell what life is like, or pretend to be an organ in the body and describe a typical day.

★ Give your child a chance to speak into a tape recorder on one of the following topics or another you think of—"Questions I'm thinking about," "New understandings about life," or "Things I feel"—as a result of something he is studying.

★ Before your child starts her homework, have her list personal questions that she can apply to the homework; after she completes the homework, have her look at the questions again and add or delete questions as appropriate.

Story Grid for Creative Writing

Hero	Villain	Conflict	Setting	Ending

4

Activities for Reflective Use of the Intelligences

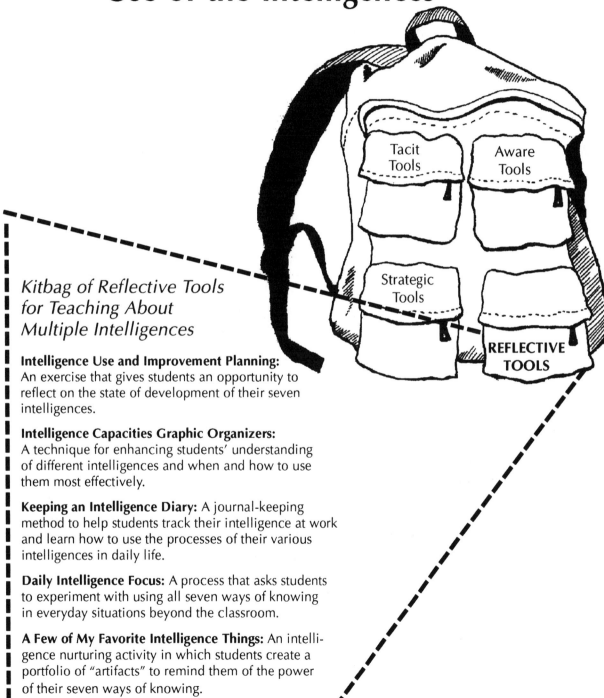

Kitbag of Reflective Tools for Teaching About Multiple Intelligences

Intelligence Use and Improvement Planning: An exercise that gives students an opportunity to reflect on the state of development of their seven intelligences.

Intelligence Capacities Graphic Organizers: A technique for enhancing students' understanding of different intelligences and when and how to use them most effectively.

Keeping an Intelligence Diary: A journal-keeping method to help students track their intelligence at work and learn how to use the processes of their various intelligences in daily life.

Daily Intelligence Focus: A process that asks students to experiment with using all seven ways of knowing in everyday situations beyond the classroom.

A Few of My Favorite Intelligence Things: An intelligence nurturing activity in which students create a portfolio of "artifacts" to remind them of the power of their seven ways of knowing.

Veronica was a sixth-grade student who, for the past two years, had teachers who used multiple intelligences as a regular part of their teaching. These teachers also worked with students regularly to help students understand as much as possible about the intelligences: how the different intelligences work (that is, the neurobiological processes involved) and how to improve or strengthen all of the intelligences. The teachers also encouraged students to use all seven ways of knowing in homework assignments, on tests, in processing lessons, in reports, and so on.

During a parent-teacher conference, Mrs. Rodriguez, Veronica's sixth-grade teacher, had a conversation with Veronica's father.

Veronica's father asked, "What is this stuff you are teaching about different intelligences? I thought your job was to teach the three Rs."

Mrs. Rodriguez responded by asking, "What has Veronica told you?"

Veronica's father related a situation that occurred in their home one evening in the last few weeks: "We were having a family discussion about how to deal with a certain problem we were facing. A fairly heated argument broke out because everyone had a different idea about what should be done. Suddenly, Veronica took over the conversation and said we needed to be thinking about the problem in more ways than just one! She said that she has learned some things in school that she thought could help us. Then she suggested that we needed not only to talk about the problem, but we should also draw pictures of it, act it out, create a song about it, and take some individual quiet time to reflect on it. We all thought she was nuts, but we were clearly not getting anywhere with the argument approach. So we tried some of the things she suggested. And you know what? It got us beyond arguing. We started listening to each other's opinions and ideas in a new way. It was really quite amazing!"

Mrs. Rodriguez responded, "Well, this is exciting to me. One of the ways I know I am teaching well is if students take what they are learning in the classroom into their everyday lives. Yes, you are right, my job is to teach the three Rs, but we have discovered that not all students learn and know in the same way. Teaching students about different ways of learning and knowing is helping them understand the three Rs much better. I'm sure you have noticed that Veronica is doing much better in school."

The father said, "Oh, don't get me wrong—I'm not complaining. I'm just very interested; her suggestions made a big difference in our discussion. And they helped us move toward a solution to the problem. I'm glad you're teaching her these things. Is there a way parents could learn about these different ways of learning too?"

Mrs. Rodriguez was able to invite Veronica's father and mother to join a school-sponsored parents' workshop dealing with multiple intelligences.

Seven Pathways of Learning © 1994 Zephyr Press, Tucson, Arizona

INTELLIGENCE USE AND IMPROVEMENT PLANNING

Lesson Procedures

1. Give each student a copy of the appropriate planning work sheet (pp. 154–55). Each student will turn to a partner and together the partners will brainstorm a list of several story characters (elementary) or historical or literary figures (middle or secondary), each of which embodies one of the intelligences. If you teach middle or secondary students, also have them brainstorm contemporary occupations that require strength in the capacities related to each intelligence. Give students ten to fifteen minutes to brainstorm with their partners.

2. Get a quick cross-section of the responses students wrote on their charts.

3. Give students ten to fifteen minutes without their partners to think of examples of situations in which the students like to use each intelligence most. They will come up with seven situations, one for each intelligence.

   Note: For the elementary level, you may need to lead students through the questions one by one, depending on verbal and writing skills. Let students draw their answers if they need to.

4. After the allotted time, have students turn to their partners and share their responses. Make sure that they discuss each situation and ask each other questions about it. As they get ideas from their partners, students may want to add to or change their responses in some or all parts of the chart; they may do so as long as the situations are still those in which the students enjoy using the intelligence. You are after honest reflection here, not conformity.

5. Have students exchange charts with their partners. Each person considers what his or her partner has said about each situation and then writes practical intelligence advice, suggesting ways the partner might use the other

Intelligence Use and Improvement Planning

INTRODUCTION

In this lesson students have the opportunity to reflect on the state of their seven intelligences. The students look into the past, consider the present, and think about the future.

OBJECTIVE

The goal of the lesson is to help students create plans for working consciously to improve their seven ways of knowing and for integrating the ways more fully into their everyday lives.

DISCUSSION

The ability to be self-reflective is unique to the human species, as far as we know. In this book we see the possibilities of this dynamic gift operating on almost every page. In some ways this lesson puts a capstone on all of the work I have been suggesting regarding the seven intelligences: how students use them and how students can strengthen them.

six intelligences to expand her or his approaches to each situation. It may help students if you give them a formula such as, "Have you considered trying . . . " or "In this situation you might think about using . . . " After they complete their writing have the partners decide which one of them will be person A and which will be person B. Person A will be the listener and person B the speaker. Have them go through the following process:

- Person B gives person A advice regarding possible other intelligent approaches to each situation person A listed.
- As person B speaks, person A listens carefully to the suggestions. Person A is not to argue or disagree, but may ask questions for clarification.
- When Person B is finished giving advice, person A thanks person B for the wise counsel.

7. Have students repeat the process with the roles reversed: person B is the listener and person A is the speaker and advice giver.
8. When the students have finished giving each other advice, have them work individually again. They will rank the suggestions they received from their partners, beginning with "things I think I may want to try next time . . . " and ending with "thank you very much, but I don't want to try that idea." For elementary levels, have each student draw the picture suggested on the work sheet.
9. Lead the whole class in the following reflection on the lesson:

- *What are some things you heard from your partner when you were the listener?*
- *What are some things you said as the speaker or advice giver?*
- *What were your feelings when your partner was giving his or her advice?*
- *What were your feelings when you were giving advice?*
- *How did this activity help you?*
- *What did you learn about yourself and your intelligences as you did this activity?*

Intelligence Use and Improvement Planning Extensions

More Intelligence Use and Improvement Planning Lesson Ideas

The following are ideas you may adapt to your academic content.

- **Setting "Intelligence Improvement" Goals.** Ask students to make two columns on a piece of paper and label the first column *Now* and the second *6 Months*. Have students write a few notes to themselves regarding their relative strengths and weaknesses in each intelligence in the *Now* column, and, in the *6 Months* column, the skills students would like to have developed in six months. Then ask them to pair off and create a plan to help them reach their six-month goals.

- **Setting "Intelligence Use" Goals.** Have students work alone to list the sections of a normal day in their lives. Have them create additional lists, one for each section of their day, that state how they use the intelligences during the different parts. Now have the students estimate the percentage of a normal day that they use each intelligence. Finally, have them create a plan for intentionally incorporating the lower percentage intelligences into their day more frequently.

- **Intelligence in the Past.** Ask students to think about their lives in the past and to list five to ten situations, events, and experiences in which the students wish they had known about the seven intelligences. After students have completed their lists, have them each turn to a neighbor and share by asking each other, "How would the seven ways of knowing possibly have made a difference in outcomes?"

- **Intelligence in the Future.** Have students consider what they think their lives will be like over the next year. Ask the students to list five to ten events they anticipate, including both exciting and difficult times. When the students have finished, have them turn to partners and share their lists. Have them ask each other, "How can your knowledge about the seven ways of knowing help you in these situations? What do you need to do to remind yourself to use all seven?"

- **The Possible Human.** Ask students each to imagine themselves as a person who has all of her or his intelligence potential fully activated. Have them list all those things in their lives that they think might be different from the way things are now. Then have students close their eyes and try to get a picture in their minds' eyes of themselves as that person. When they have a sense of that person, have them open their eyes and draw a symbol that will remind them of this possibility. Tell them to post the symbol someplace where they will see it every day.

- **Intelligent Schoolwork.** Have students make a list of the different subjects or content areas that are part of a normal day or week in school. They are to list the intelligences that they use the most when doing work related to each subject or content area. Then have them find partners and brainstorm ideas for extending the use of all seven ways of knowing in each of these curriculum areas.

Intelligence Use and Improvement Planning
(Elementary)

Think of story characters who . . .	**Think of when you . . .**
Like to talk, read, or write	Like to talk, read, or write
Like to be really active or exercise	Like to be really active or exercise
Like to solve problems	Like to solve problems
Like music, singing, or making sounds	Like music, singing, or making sounds
Like to pretend, dream, or draw	Like to pretend, dream, or draw
Like working with others	Like working with others
Like to be alone and think about stuff	Like to be alone and think about stuff

Draw someone who likes to do all of these things!

Intelligence Use and Improvement Planning
(Middle School & Secondary)

	Historical/Literary Figures	Present-Day Occupations	When I Like to Use Each Intelligence
Verbal/Linguistic			
Logical/Mathematical			
Visual/Spatial			
Bodily/Kinesthetic			
Musical/Rhythmic			
Interpersonal			
Intrapersonal			

Notes on my partner's advice:

Teacher's Personal Reflection Log

INTELLIGENCE USE AND IMPROVEMENT PLANNING

I have the following thoughts/insights about the Intelligence Use and Improvement Planning strategy:

I feel that the Intelligence Use and Improvement Planning strategy can help me in my teaching in the following ways:

As a learning process, the Intelligence Use and Improvement Planning strategy includes the following benefits for my students:

I have the following specific ideas for using the Intelligence Use and Improvement Planning strategy in my classroom in the near future:

I think the Intelligence Use and Improvement Planning strategy can be used beyond the classroom and school in the following ways:

INTELLIGENCE CAPACITIES GRAPHIC ORGANIZERS

Lesson Procedures

This lesson is really four separate mini-lessons, each one using a different graphic organizer to analyze the capacities of the different intelligences. Each section outlined below constitutes one such graphic organizer lesson. See the grade-appropriate examples on pages 161–62.

Mini-Lesson 1: Intelligence Analysis Using a Web

1. Introduce students to webbing by leading them in a practice exercise using things within the classroom: defining the characteristics of clothes, the attributes of the overhead projector, and so on.
2. Have students get into seven groups. Students will be in the same group throughout the four lessons in this activity. Assign each group one of the seven intelligences.
3. Students are to draw a web on a piece of newsprint and list on the rays of the web as many of the defining attributes of their assigned intelligence as they can think of.

Intelligence Capacities Graphic Organizers

INTRODUCTION

This lesson is designed to help students understand the various capacities or skills of the seven intelligences more fully, so that students can decide when to use which intelligence to achieve certain goals in everyday life.

OBJECTIVE

The goal of this lesson is to help students clearly define the capacities and skills that are related to each intelligence using cognitive or graphic organizers.

DISCUSSION

Cognitive research indicates very clearly the power of using graphic or cognitive organizers to teach students thinking skills. One reason these organizers are so effective is that they are in synch with how the brain organizes and processes information: in a hierarchical manner moving from general concepts to the specific parts and pieces. A graphic organizer simply helps us make this process visible so that we can work with the process, enhance it, and use it with greater consciousness and intention. My adaptation of graphic organizers to the intelligences focuses first on creating an awareness of the different capacities we all have as human beings, and second on ways to integrate this awareness into daily living. The more we learn about our different ways of knowing (be they seven or seventy), the more we can bring our full intellectual potential to bear on solving the problems and dealing with the challenges facing our planet today.

4. When students have completed this task, have them put a star by the critical attributes of their assigned intelligence, the attributes that are most important and unique to that intelligence.

5. Post and discuss the webs (see discussion suggestions at the end of these procedures).

Mini-Lesson 2: Intelligence Analysis Using a Triangle Chart

1. Introduce students to the triangle chart by leading them in a practice exercise: do something, such as taking a bite out of an apple, and have the class brainstorm what it looks like, sounds like, and feels like.

2. Have students get in their groups. Assign each group one of the seven intelligences, making sure that each group is working on a different intelligence from the one they worked on in the first mini-lesson.

3. Have each group make a triangle chart on a piece of newsprint and have them brainstorm as much information as they can on what it looks like (what they see when this intelligence is in operation), what it sounds like (the sounds they hear when this intelligence is being used), and what it feels like (the emotional responses they associate with this intelligence).

4. Post and discuss the triangle charts (see discussion suggestions at the end of these procedures).

Mini-Lesson 3: Intelligence Analysis Using a Matrix

1. Introduce students to the use of a matrix by leading them in a practice exercise: show the class several items or pictures and have the students classify the items based on certain criteria (color, size, shape, material, use, and so on).

2. Have students get into their groups. Assign each group to work on one of the seven intelligences, making sure that each group is working on a different intelligence from the two they worked on in the previous mini-lessons.

3. Each group is to make an intelligence matrix on a piece of newsprint using categories such as those in the examples. The groups fill in the various boxes of the matrix with as much information as they can related to the operation and uses of the assigned intelligences.

4. Post and discuss the matrixes (see discussion suggestions at the end of these procedures).

Seven Pathways of Learning © 1994 Zephyr Press, Tucson, Arizona

Mini-Lesson 4: Intelligence Analysis Using a Venn Diagram

1. Introduce students to the Venn diagram by having them practice comparing and contrasting various things in the classroom: the people sitting on one side of the room to the people on the other, for example.
2. Have students get into their groups. Each group will focus on one of the seven intelligences. Make sure they are working on a different intelligence from the three they worked on in the previous mini-lessons.
3. Have each group make six Venn diagrams on a piece of newsprint. Next have the students label each Venn with their assigned intelligence in the left circle and each of the other intelligence in each right circle and proceed to compare and contrast their assigned intelligence with each of the other six intelligences. Similarities will go in the overlapping sections of the diagram; differences will go in the separate parts of the circles. If the group was assigned musical/ rhythmic intelligence, for example, the first Venn would compare and contrast musical/rhythmic intelligence and bodily/kinesthetic, the next would be musical/rhythmic and visual/spatial, and so on.
4. Post and discuss the Venn diagrams when they are completed (see discussion suggestions at the end of these procedures).

General Discussion to Follow Each Mini-Lesson

Ask the class to make general observations as they look at the different graphic organizers: similarities (things that show up on two or more charts), uniqueness (things that are on only one of the charts), and so on. Ask the following questions:

- *What do you find especially interesting about the charts? What is exciting about them? What confuses you?*
- *What new insights into the seven ways of knowing do these charts give you?*

Give students a few minutes to write in their journals a response to the question, "What new ideas do I have about how to use the intelligences in my everyday life beyond school?"

Intelligence Capacities
Graphic Organizers Extensions

More Intelligence Capacities Graphic Organizers Lesson Ideas

The following are ideas you may adapt to your academic content. See examples on page 163.

- **Intelligent Ranking Ladder.** Begin by having students rank the intelligences in several ways: from favorite to least favorite, strongest to weakest, one they need to work on most to one they need to work on least. Have students talk with three other students and notice the similarities and differences among their rankings. Lead the class in a discussion about the discoveries they made about themselves and about each other.

- **Applied Intelligence Snapshots.** Have students create a set of ideas for using the intelligences beyond the classroom, one set for each intelligence. Students should try to come up with very practical ideas that one could take snapshots of. When students have completed one set of snapshots, have them share their ideas with each other.

- **KWL.** Have each student create a chart with three columns. The students will label the first column "Know" (things I know about the intelligences), the second "Want to Know" (things I want to know), and the third "Learned" (things I have learned about the seven ways of knowing). Give them a few minutes to work on listing items in the first two columns. Ask them to turn to a partner and share items from the first two columns. When they are through sharing, create a class KWL chart and leave it posted. Add to the "L" column as appropriate.

- **Intelligence Thought Tree.** Have students put the name of one of the intelligences in the top box of a tree organizer. In the next row of boxes, students will start making associations with the intelligence, then in the next row, they will make associations with the associations. Tell students to try making one thought tree for each intelligence, then to compare the associations from the different thought trees.

- **PNI.** Give students time to evaluate each of the seven ways of knowing by having them write about the positive points of each intelligence (P), about the negative points (N), and about what they find interesting about each (I). Have several volunteers share their thoughts with the rest of the class. Note the feelings and thoughts common to some or all of the volunteers' lists.

Intelligence Capacities Graphic Organizers
(Elementary)

WEB

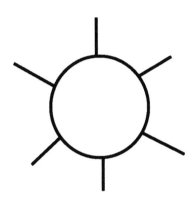

What do you do when you're using this way of knowing?

TRIANGLE

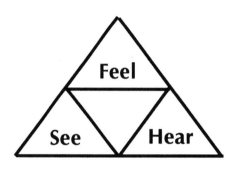

- **Tell what you see**
- **Tell what you hear**
- **Tell what you feel**

CHART

Seeing	Reading	Drawing
Speaking	Action	Writing
Listening	Touching	Thinking

Make an "X" in each box that is true for your way of knowing

VENN

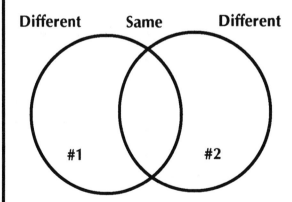

How are two ways of knowing the same and different?

Intelligence Capacities Graphic Organizers
(Middle School & Secondary)

ATTRIBUTE WEB

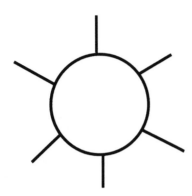

1. **List the attributes of your assigned intelligence on the rays of the web.**
2. **Put an asterisk (*) by the attributes that are unique to this intelligence.**

TRIANGLE CHART

For your assigned intelligence list
- the "looks like" (what you see)
- the "sounds like" (what you hear)
- the "feels like" (what you feel, your emotions)

CLASSIFICATION MATRIX

Intelligence:

	In School	In the Community	In the World
In Myself			
In Friends			
In Others			

1. **Study and discuss the top and side categories on the matrix.**
2. **Fill in the center boxes with examples of the intelligences that honor the top and side intersections.**

VENN DIAGRAM

Assigned Intelligence: **Comparing Intelligence:**

1. **On the left and right, list ways your assigned intelligence and another intelligence are different from each other.**
2. **In the middle, list ways in which they are similar.**

More Graphic Organizers
(All Grades)

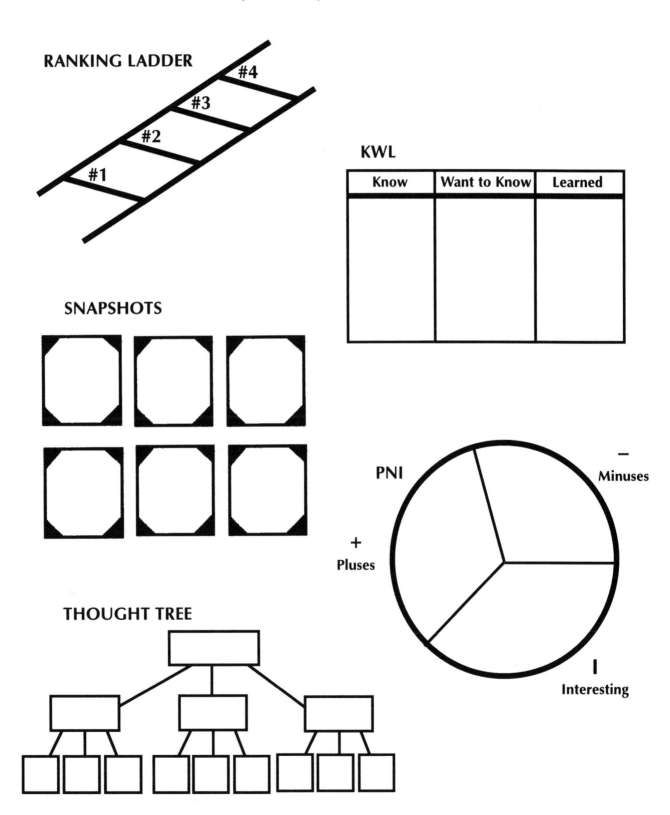

RANKING LADDER

#4
#3
#2
#1

KWL

Know	Want to Know	Learned

SNAPSHOTS

PNI

− **Minuses**

+ **Pluses**

I **Interesting**

THOUGHT TREE

Teacher's Personal Reflection Log
INTELLIGENCE CAPACITIES GRAPHIC ORGANIZERS

I have the following thoughts/insights about the Graphic Organizers strategy:

I feel that the Graphic Organizers strategy can help me in my teaching in the following ways:

As a learning process, the Graphic Organizers strategy includes the following benefits for my students:

I have the following specific ideas for using the Graphic Organizers strategy in my classroom in the near future:

I think the Graphic Organizers strategy can be used beyond the classroom and school in the following ways:

Seven Pathways of Learning © 1994 Zephyr Press, Tucson, Arizona

KEEPING AN INTELLIGENCE DIARY

Lesson Procedures

1. Give each student a special notebook or folder that is to be an Intelligence Diary. Tell students they are to reflect on their intelligences each day and to make an entry about their reflections in their diaries. They will make entries for one month.

2. Introduce students to the appropriate reflection models in the examples (pp. 168–169) or other models you think of. Suggest that your students try a variety of reflective approaches during the course of the month. Following are instructions for using each model shown.

   - **Model 1:** Provide a series of "finish this phrase" *writing* stems or lead-ins to help students get started. Students are to write their responses to one or more of the phrases in their Intelligence Diaries.

   - **Model 2:** Create a set of doing stems for students to use to reflect on the day or on a particular lesson. These stems are lead-ins, like those above, but they ask students to do more than just write about the day. Make sure that the stems require students to use all seven intelligences to respond.

   - **Model 3:** This model suggests that students pretend their intelligences are animals (elementary) or people (middle or secondary). The students also pretend they can converse with the animals or people. To prepare for the process, students should create some questions they would like to ask their intelligences. During the pretending part of the exercise, students should record the answers they get from the different intelligences.

   - **Model 4:** Encourage students to invent new models and approaches to reflect on the day or on a particular lesson. The

---

Keeping an Intelligence Diary

INTRODUCTION

This lesson helps students foster a metacognitive awareness of their own intelligence processes. Students will learn a variety of journaling techniques by which they can become more skilled at tracking their intelligences.

OBJECTIVE

The goal of this lesson is to introduce students to the discipline of keeping a journal or log and to catalyze in them an interest to do so.

DISCUSSION

Keeping a journal or log is a powerful tool of transformation. By their very nature, journals cause one to be introspective, and that very introspection has the potential to open new realms of thought and experience. As we become aware of ourselves, and, in a sense, take a step back and watch ourselves, we gain new power over our lives. We are much less likely to abdicate responsibility for our actions. We are less apt to fall into the feeling that we are victims of someone else's decisions. And we are less likely to get stuck in various kinds of habitual, robotlike behavior patterns.

Following are some keys to keeping journals, logs, or diaries successfully: (1) write entries on a regular basis (daily or every other day); (2) make the exercise fun, creative, and relaxing so that you will look forward to it; (3) get a special notebook and special recording media (colored pens, markers, paints, clay, tape recorder, construction paper, and so on); and (4) do your writing in a special place (where you will not be disturbed for five to ten minutes) and at a special time of the day (generally at its end).

manner in which students reflect is not important; that they reflect is extremely important. Just make sure that the students document what they did and what they learned.

3. Once a week, ask students to share what is happening and what they are learning as they keep their Intelligence Diaries. Following are some examples of questions you may use:

   • *Will some of you volunteer to share one entry from your diaries? Let's try to get a variety of types of entries, such as something you've written, drawn, sung, and so on.*

   • *What are your feelings about this assignment? Did you like it? Why or why not?*

   • *What are you learning about yourself as you reflect in this way each day?*

   • *What tips can you give to others about how to make journaling go easier? How to make it more fun? Other approaches to the task you have invented?*

Keeping an Intelligence Diary Extensions

More Keeping an Intelligence Diary Lesson Ideas

The following are ideas you may adapt to your academic content.

• **The Montage Journal.** Give students a sheet of heavy paper, magazines with lots of pictures, scissors, and glue. Tell the students they are to create an all-pictures reflection on a particular lesson. Tell them to remember that the colors they choose can also communicate their feelings and thoughts.

• **The Audiocassette Log.** Allow students to speak their thoughts into a tape recorder. You might try a format such as an "Oprah Winfrey" talk show where you or other students interview each other to get reflections on a lesson or on the day.

• **Sculpting, Painting, or Drawing Your Reflections.** Give students clay, paints, or colored markers and instruct them to create a visual expression of their thoughts and feelings. The expression can be a literal picture or simply a series of designs, shapes, and colors. The key to this process is getting students to trust their intuition and their first impulse of what they want to make.

• **The Sounds and Music of the Day.** Have each student create a chart that shows the different parts of his or her day. Then have students decide the appropriate sound and music that they would play to accompany each segment. Once they have orchestrated their day, have them pair with partners and share the sounds and music of the day.

Seven Pathways of Learning © 1994 Zephyr Press, Tucson, Arizona

- **The Kinesthetic Journal.** Ask each student to make up a short pantomime or charade that says through body language what he or she thinks or feels about a lesson. Then have the students perform their dramas one at a time for the class, with the rest of the class trying to guess what the performer said in and through the drama.

- **Reflections through Poetry.** Teach students the structure of a limerick and then have each student create a limerick that shares thoughts and feelings about a lesson. Get a random sampling of limericks for the whole class to enjoy. You could also work with other poetry forms such as haiku, free verse, sonnets, and so on.

- **A Story about a Unit.** Assign students the task of writing "Once upon a time . . . " short stories about a unit you have just completed. The story should follow the structure of a classical story. Tell students to be creative and playful with their stories. When students have finished writing, have a story-reading session.

- **Naming the Patterns of the Day.** Have students create a time line of the previous day, beginning with the time they woke up and ending with the time they went to bed. Then ask them to list key events and to plot the events at the appropriate place on the time line. Next have the students look back over the day for patterns (that is, groupings of events) or divisions in the day. Have them create titles for these groupings or for the different segments of the day.

Keeping an Intelligence Diary
(Elementary)

MODEL 1
Stems (writing)

I wanted to sing when . . .

Today I used my body to . . .

It was fun today when . . .

It was hard today when . . .

Something I made today was . . .

I talked with a friend about . . .

I felt really smart today when . . .

It really made me think when . . .

I wanted to be alone today when . . .

Something I read today was . . .

I used numbers today for . . .

MODEL 2
More stems (doing)

Draw something from the day.

Make up a song about today.

Do an action from the day.

Talk to a partner about the day.

Make a rhyme about the day.

Paint the colors of your day.

Beat out the rhythms of your day.

Be silent and remember the day.

Act out how you feel about today.

Make sounds you heard today.

MODEL 3

**What is your favorite
way of knowing?**

**What kind of animal
would it be?**

**Pretend you can talk to
your "knowing animal."
What would it say?**

**What would your
"knowing animal"
say or ask you?**

MODEL 4

**Make something
to remind you
of what you
learned today.**

168

Keeping an Intelligence Diary
(Middle School & Secondary)

MODEL 1
Journal Writing Starters

- *I used my _____ intelligence most today in the following situations:*

- *I had the most trouble using _____ intelligence today because . . .*

- *The time today when I used the most intelligences at the same time was . . .*

- *Something I learned today about how I think and learn was . . .*

- *I had the most fun today when I was using my _____ intelligence because . . .*

- *A new idea I had about how all seven ways of knowing can help me in my life is . . .*

- *The biggest difficulty I'm having using my seven ways of knowing is . . .*

MODEL 2
Journal Doing Starters

- *An image or picture I have of this day is . . .* (Draw it.)

- *If today were a song, it would be . . .* (Sing it.)

- *My inner feelings about today are . . .* (Meditate on it.)

- *A body movement or gesture for today is . . .* (Do it.)

- *A thought I've had today is . . .* (Write it.)

- *I want to talk with someone about . . .* (Discuss it.)

- *A thought pattern I find interesting is . . .* (Think about it.)

MODEL 3
A Chat with My Intelligence

1. Pretend your seven intelligences are seven people you can talk to. Close your eyes and imagine what they look like.

2. Now pretend that you are having a chat with them. Spend a minute with each of these "intelligence persons" and ask them each a question.

3. Imagine you hear them answering your questions. What is their message for you? (Remember that their answers may not be in words!)

4. In your journal, write what happened. What did your intelligences communicate to you that you want to remember?

5. Turn to a person sitting near you and share what happened.

MODEL 3
Inventing New Journaling Ideas

Make up seven new ideas for reflecting on the day—one idea for each intelligence.

Teacher's Personal Reflection Log

KEEPING AN INTELLIGENCE DIARY

I have the following thoughts/insights about the Intelligence Diary strategy:

I feel that the Intelligence Diary strategy can help me in my teaching in the following ways:

As a learning process, the Intelligence Diary strategy includes the following benefits for my students:

I have the following specific ideas for using the Intelligence Diary strategy in my classroom in the near future:

I think the Intelligence Diary strategy can be used beyond the classroom and school in the following ways:

Seven Pathways of Learning © 1994 Zephyr Press, Tucson, Arizona

DAILY INTELLIGENCE FOCUS

Lesson Procedures

1. Pass out a copy of the appropriate intelligence weekly planner (pp. 174–75) to each student. Say, *"The lesson we are about to start will take one week to complete. You will choose an intelligence to focus on for each day of the coming week. You'll then have some time to create a plan in which you will include every way you can think of to incorporate the day's intelligence into all that you do."*

2. Explain how to use the weekly planner:

   - Before beginning, students will work on their own and draw a picture or image (elementary) or write the name of an intelligence (middle and secondary) in the space provided for each day of the week. Each day is to have a different intelligence focus. As the days come up, students will focus on the intelligence they have listed.

   - After students have finished listing the focuses, ask the students how they decided which intelligence to assign to which day. Was their choice random, or did they have a rationale?

   - Now have students list at least seven ideas, one for each day, of what they will do to implement the assigned focus.

   - After each person has come up with one idea for each day, have her or him turn to a partner; the partners will share ideas, and both will come up with one more idea for each day.

   - Have students thank their partners and find other partners. With the new partners they are to repeat the process, coming up with one more idea for each day. At the end of these two rounds of working with a partner, each student will have at least three ideas for each day.

   Note: Stress to your students that *it's okay to steal ideas from each other!*

Daily Intelligence Focus

INTRODUCTION

In this lesson students are assigned to focus on different intelligence skills and capacities each day of the week. The students are asked to experiment with using the intelligences consciously in new situations.

OBJECTIVE

The goal of the lesson is to help students transfer their knowledge about the intelligences into the task of daily living beyond the classroom.

DISCUSSION

In some ways the intelligences are like any skills or capacities we have—the more we use them, the better they become. We often let ourselves fall into various kinds of routine patterns of behavior and thinking. As a matter of course, we generally do not venture into areas that require risk and with which we are uncomfortable. We often prefer the so-called tried and true over the new and uncertain. The Daily Intelligence Focus lesson is a way to interrupt this propensity, thus giving students (and teachers!) a way to step beyond the predictable boredom of "every day is the same as the day before." Not only can this exercise make each day more interesting, it can strengthen all of our intelligence capacities, many of which will not get exercised if we are simply left to our regular routines.

- Have students thank each other for the ideas and then pull the class back together as a whole group.

3. Lead students in the following sharing discussion:
    - *Who would like to share some of the great ideas he or she got from a partner?*
    - *Look at your own planning work sheet and pick the day you think is the most interesting. What are you going to try that day?*
    - *Pick the day that looks most boring or predictable. Share your ideas for that day. Ask the whole class for other ideas that could "juice up" that day so it isn't so boring and predictable.*
    - *Which day are you looking forward to the most? Why?*

4. Say, "*A part of your homework assignment each day is to spend five minutes reflecting on the day and reviewing the ideas you tried. The most important part of the lesson is this debriefing at the end of the day. Write what happened, how you felt, and what you learned as you focused on and experimented with the intelligence of the day.*"

5. At the end of the week, schedule a time for students to share what happened and what they learned about their intelligences. Ask students if they would like to continue the lesson for another week.

Daily Intelligence Focus Extensions

More Daily Intelligence Focus Lesson Ideas

The following are ideas you may adapt to your academic content.

- **TV Watching with a Focus.** Assign students to experiment with watching TV shows or videos with part of their attention "tracking" the occurrences of the seven intelligences: music, sounds, colors, settings and props, relationships, and so on. The students are then to write a short report on their observations about how the producers used the intelligences and to what ends.

- **Sorting the News.** Assign students to read a newspaper or news magazine and sort the stories into the seven intelligence areas. You could also have them look for the seven intelligences within a single article; students would be reading between the lines for the "intelligence news"! Remember the intelligence news may not be the same as the news being overtly reported in the article.

- **Fine-Tuning Intelligence Capacities.** Assign students a one-week experiment in which they pretend that their various intelligence capacities or skills are on a rheostat or dial that can be turned higher or lower at will. Each day of the week focus on one intelligence and have your students experiment with turning that intelligence up and down. At the end of the week ask students to share their experiences and learnings with each other.

Seven Pathways of Learning © 1994 Zephyr Press, Tucson, Arizona

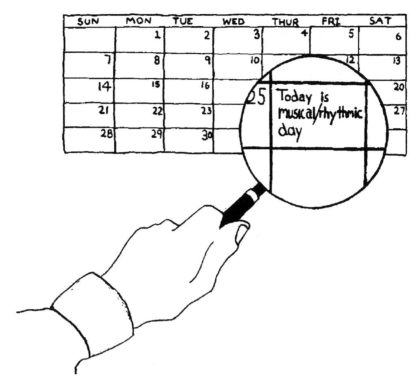

- **People Watching with an Intelligent Eye**. Assign students to experiment with watching people involved in various group situations. Ask students to keep a log of what they learned about people's intelligence strengths and weaknesses just by carefully observing behavior through the eyeglasses of multiple intelligences. Suggest such situations as people on a crowded bus, people standing in a line at the supermarket, people coming out of a theater after a movie, and so on.

- **Focus to Foci**. Provide an opportunity for students to experience typical art forms created by various intelligences: painting or sculpture, a symphony, a dance, a poem, and so on. Ask students to focus their full attention on the art form and to be aware of what else is catalyzed by these art forms: other times and places in the students' lives, other people, pets, food, feelings, images, and so on.

- **Listening with All the Intelligences**. Have students take notes when they are listening to a lecture in school, a sermon in church, or a talk on TV. Students should note what the speaker is saying. They should also include the following: images or pictures, song titles or sounds—related to what the speaker is saying—that come to their minds; notes about physical gestures that could "embody" the thoughts the speaker is communicating; humorous comments they would like to make; and questions they would like to ask.

Daily Intelligence Focus
(Elementary)

How will you be smart each day?

MONDAY	TUESDAY	WEDNESDAY	THURSDAY	FRIDAY
Make a picture of Monday's way:	Make a picture of Tuesday's way:	Make a picture of Wednesday's way:	Make a picture of Thursday's way:	Make a picture of Friday's way:
IDEAS: What will I do or try?	IDEAS: What will I do or try?	IDEAS: What will I do or try?	IDEAS: What will I do or try?	IDEAS: What will I do or try?

Seven Ways of Being Smart

Words, language, and speech	Counting and finding patterns	Drawing, sculpting, and painting	Body movement and action	Singing, sounds, and drumming	Talking and listening to others	Being alone and thinking

Seven Pathways of Learning © 1994 Zephyr Press, Tucson, Arizona

Daily Intelligence Focus
(Middle School & Secondary)

My plan for being intelligent this week

MONDAY	TUESDAY	WEDNESDAY	THURSDAY	FRIDAY
Intelligence focus:	Intelligence focus:	Intelligence focus:	Intelligence focus:	Intelligence focus:
IDEAS: What will I do or try?	IDEAS: What will I do or try?	IDEAS: What will I do or try?	IDEAS: What will I do or try?	IDEAS: What will I do or try?
1.	1.	1.	1.	1.
2.	2.	2.	2.	2.
3.	3.	3.	3.	3.
4.	4.	4.	4.	4.
5.	5.	5.	5.	5.

Seven Ways of Being Smart

Verbal/ Linguistic	Logical/ Mathematical	Visual/ Spatial	Bodily/ Kinesthetic	Musical/ Rhythmic	Inter- personal	Intra- personal

Seven Pathways of Learning © 1994 Zephyr Press, Tucson, Arizona

Teacher's Personal Reflection Log

DAILY INTELLIGENCE FOCUS

I have the following thoughts/insights about the Daily Intelligence Focus strategy:

I feel that the Daily Intelligence Focus strategy can help me in my teaching in the following ways:

As a learning process, the Daily Intelligence Focus strategy includes the following benefits for my students:

I have the following specific ideas for using the Daily Intelligence Focus strategy in my classroom in the near future:

I think the Daily Intelligence Focus strategy can be used beyond the classroom and school in the following ways:

Seven Pathways of Learning © 1994 Zephyr Press, Tucson, Arizona

A FEW OF MY FAVORITE INTELLIGENCE THINGS

Lesson Procedures

1. Ask students to bring a medium-sized box to class. On the day you begin this lesson, introduce the idea of an "intelligence kitbag" to the class by saying,

   > Over the next three weeks you will be putting various things into the box. You will choose things that help you be aware of and use all seven ways of knowing, both in your studies and in your life beyond the classroom. This box will become your multiple intelligences kitbag. The kitbag is like a doctor's bag, which contains the basic tools he or she needs to be a good doctor. The intelligence kitbag contains tools, techniques, methods, and so on that you need to be the most intelligent person you can be! It may also contain examples of things you and others have produced using the different intelligences. It should contain items that are reminders of your multiple intelligence capabilities as well as items that are somehow inspiring to you.

2. Begin by giving students time to cover and decorate their boxes. You want students to invest some time and energy in creating their kitbags so that the boxes will have the students' personal touches and will remind the students' of their seven ways of knowing as soon as they see the boxes! Make sure that you have all the materials on hand for students to decorate their kitbags: paints, colored markers, colored paper, and so on.

   Note: In the next step of the lesson, you will be asked to show students your kitbag as an example. So if you haven't created one yet, now is an excellent time to do so!

3. Show students your intelligence kitbag, displaying the items and explaining why the

A Few of My Favorite Intelligence Things

INTRODUCTION

This lesson asks students to create a kitbag that contains their favorite tools and techniques for each of the seven intelligences, the ones they enjoy using most. The lesson is most appropriate after students have a fair degree of familiarity with the intelligences and have been working with them for some time.

OBJECTIVE

The goal of this lesson is to help students create tangible evidence of the power and benefit of the seven ways of knowing, and to catalyze a deep resolve to integrate the intelligences into their everyday living.

DISCUSSION

Many of our cultural traditions have taught us the importance of symbols in our lives. Human beings are symbol-making creatures. We live by our symbols. They tell us who we are and what we are doing with our lives and why. They communicate the meaning and purpose of our existence. In this lesson, students are asked to create a kitbag that contains items that symbolize for them the seven ways of knowing. The very act of collecting the items will be profoundly important to many students, for they are not only putting things in their kitbags that remind them of the seven intelligences, but at some deep, unconscious level, they are symbolizing their full potential as human beings. The objects they choose will likely be things that evoke many latent potentials that can provide a deeper, fuller, and richer experience of living.

kitbag is important to you and how it helps remind you of the seven intelligences.

4. Ask students to brainstorm a list of items that represent the different intelligences and that they might want to include in their kitbags (see suggestions in the examples on pp. 181–82 to "prime the pump" as needed). Ask students to think about the following questions to get started:

   - *What are the tools, techniques, strategies, and methods for each intelligence that work best for you?* (Responses should be things that get the students into the modality of each intelligence quickly: a favorite audiotape, a set of colored marking pens, a Rubik's cube, a book of poetry, and so on.)
   - *What things could you put into the kitbag that would symbolize for you the different ways of knowing?* (Responses should symbolize and call to mind the essence of each of the intelligences: how it operates, its unique language, its core capacities, how to trigger it in the brain, and so on.)
   - *What things could you include, which you have produced or created, as examples of your different intelligences at work?* (Students should include artifacts that, when the students see them, will remind the students of their multiple intelligence capacities.)

5. After students have some ideas of what they *might* include in their kitbags, tell them that they have three weeks to work on creating their kitbags. They are to have at least one item for each intelligence. At the end of the three weeks they will have an opportunity to share what is in their kitbags with other students.

6. Kitbag sharing:

   - Place students into groups of three or four.
   - Have the students in each group proceed in round-robin fashion, with students sharing in turn what items they put in their kitbags and how they plan to use those items. Have each student explain why she or he chose particular items and tell how she or he plans to use those items. It is best to deal with one intelligence at a time, with each student in the group sharing the items she or he has collected for one intelligence before moving on to the next intelligence. Sharing in this way keeps the conversation more lively and interesting because students will go around the group seven times.

7. Consider setting up individual student-teacher conferences to go through students' kitbags with them.

   - Compare your and your students' notes on what you have observed the students doing as they were involved in various learning activities, and comment on the items they have included in their kitbags.

- Make additional suggestions of things students may want to consider including in the kitbag.

Note: This conference is a great opportunity to reflect with students on the development of their own intelligence capacities. Offer any advice you may have on exercises and practices that could help the students capitalize on their strengths and strengthen their weaker intelligences.

- Make suggestions for extending the intelligences into situations beyond the formal academic world: relationships with peers, family, resolving conflicts, and so on.
- Share your own struggles and breakthroughs in working with the intelligences.
- Let students know of your concern and support to help them develop their full intellectual potential.

A Few of My Favorite Intelligence Things Extensions

More A Few of my Favorite Intelligence Things Lesson Ideas

The following are ideas you may adapt to your academic content.

- **"Once upon an Intelligence . . . "** Have students make up an adventure story in which the hero is a fully actualized, multiple intelligence being. You might begin by having the whole class brainstorm ideas, such as various settings for the story, a conflict or challenge around which to build the story, possible endings, and so on. Give the students time to write and share their stories.

- **Multiple Intelligences Daily Ritual.** Help students create a quick rehearsal of the seven ways of knowing that they could do every day to remind themselves to use all of their intelligences. The ritual should involve things that are typical of the modality for each intelligence: drawing something, making sounds or singing, moving, and so on.

- **Personal Art Gallery.** Give students an opportunity to create art they could put on the wall of their bedrooms, works that the students think would remind them of the seven intelligences. For example, students may find or create a picture or clay object for each intelligence, or include other objects they find or acquire.

- **Personal Orchestra.** Place students in groups of three or four and have them brainstorm pieces of music that they feel are appropriate for each of the intelligences. The music should remind students of the seven ways of knowing; that is, it should communicate what each intelligence is like: "I Get Around" by the Beach Boys for bodily/kinesthetic intelligence, "I Want to Hold Your Hand" by the Beatles for interpersonal intelligence, for example.

- **Intelligence Gestures.** Have students get into groups of three or four. Have them create a hand signal or gesture, like sign language, for each of the intelligences. Have the groups share and teach their hand signals or gestures to the rest of the class. Suggest to students that they use the hand signals during the day to help them remember to use their full intellectual potential.

- **Intelligence Hero Biographies.** Assign students to create a booklet that contains at least seven biographical sketches, one for each intelligence. Have students choose at least one person (famous or otherwise, historical or fictional) that for them embodies one of the intelligence areas. Students should try to get a photo of each person they choose, an example of something the person produced or created, and a brief outline of her or his life (things that influenced her or him, family situation, special experiences, and so on). Have students repeat the process for each of the intelligences.

A Few of My Favorite Things
(All Grades)
SUGGESTIONS FOR PERSONAL INTELLIGENCE KITBAGS

Verbal/Linguistic

Tools/Techniques/Strategies/Methods
- ★ new, strange, or fun vocabulary words
- ★ humor: puns, jokes
- ★ oral or written expression of ideas
- ★ academic debate
- ★ storytelling or hearing stories

Symbols of Verbal/Linguistic Knowing
- ★ a favorite piece or book of poetry
- ★ a famous speech that "changed things"
- ★ examples of glorious metaphors or similies
- ★ a clever story with a surprise ending
- ★ a complex verbal puzzle

Creative Examples (personal)
- ★ an essay you wrote that you still like
- ★ an important poem you wrote
- ★ an award for public speaking
- ★ a really good story you can tell
- ★ a debate you won

Logical/Mathematical

Tools/Techniques/Strategies/Methods
- ★ mind-stretching puzzles or activities
- ★ finding interesting patterns in the ordinary
- ★ creating number patterns to stump others
- ★ work to solve a problem
- ★ learn new thinking patterns

Symbols of Logical/Mathematical Knowing
- ★ a catalogue of cognitive organizers
- ★ pictures of famous problem solvers
- ★ the most exciting pattern you know
- ★ formulas that have changed the world
- ★ a montage of math symbols

Creative Examples (personal)
- ★ the most difficult problem you have solved
- ★ a list of times when you need math in your life
- ★ steps of your problem-solving method
- ★ successful attempts at doing math
- ★ some clever thinking you've done

Visual/Spatial

Tools/Techniques/Strategies/Methods
- ★ a box of paints or colored marking pens
- ★ a box of modeling clay
- ★ an example of the mind-mapping process
- ★ gestalt-shift images or puzzles
- ★ an effective active imagination process

Symbols of Visual/Spatial Knowing
- ★ a favorite picture or piece of sculpture
- ★ a montage of favorite colors
- ★ a three-dimensional image or a hologram
- ★ an object that is meaningful to you
- ★ an unusual or interesting map or diagram

Creative Examples (personal)
- ★ something you've drawn
- ★ a painting you have done
- ★ something you made from clay
- ★ an intriguing pattern or design you created
- ★ a collage of different textures or touches

Bodily/Kinesthetic

Tools/Techniques/Strategies/Methods
- ★ physical exercise (dancing, jogging)
- ★ different kinds of walking
- ★ role-playing or acting out
- ★ sports and physical activities
- ★ inventing or making something

Symbols of Bodily/Kinesthetic Knowing
- ★ action pictures or posters
- ★ video of a fine physical performance
- ★ picture of a bodily/kinesthetic hero
- ★ list of favorite body language gestures
- ★ list of favorite action-packed movies

Creative Examples (personal)
- ★ an award for physical accomplishment
- ★ a picture of you doing something great
- ★ your personal exercise routine
- ★ a video of a dance you created
- ★ a program from a play you were in

Seven Pathways of Learning © 1994 Zephyr Press, Tucson, Arizona

A Few of My Favorite Things
(All Grades)
SUGGESTIONS FOR PERSONAL INTELLIGENCE KITBAGS

Musical/Rhythmic

Tools/Techniques/Strategies/Methods
★ various kinds or styles of music tapes
★ a tape of interesting sounds
★ a tape of various kinds of beats or rhythms
★ a chart of when you like what music
★ a tape of sounds from the environment

Symbols of Musical/Rhythmic Knowing
★ examples of the use of music in society
★ sounds you make in order to communicate
★ things you have learned by putting them to music
★ a list of music that alters your moods
★ a list of favorite music and why you like it

Creative Examples (personal)
★ a song or tune you wrote
★ your use of music to express yourself
★ a song you can play, sing, or hum
★ your part of a musical creation
★ a program from a musical performance you were in

Intrapersonal

Tools/Techniques/Strategies/Methods
★ self-reflection experiences
★ awareness of feelings and emotions
★ "who am I" questioning investigations
★ transpersonal sense of the self methods
★ higher-order thinking or reasoning skills

Symbols of Intrapersonal Knowing
★ personal identity symbols
★ personal goals, objectives, or directions
★ a list of personal heroes
★ a list of key personal values or beliefs
★ your technique for inner renewal

Creative Examples (personal)
★ personal goals or objectives you have attained
★ times you have trusted your intuition
★ your most creative accomplishments
★ moments when you had acute mindfulness
★ moments of deep concentration

Interpersonal

Tools/Techniques/Strategies/Methods
★ good person-to-person communication
★ positive group interdependence
★ genuine empathy with others
★ effective cooperative behavior
★ team spirit or identity "gimmicks"

Symbols of Interpersonal Knowing
★ a product of a team effort
★ example of team support or encouragement
★ consensus-building procedures
★ checklist of an "effective team"
★ pictures of exemplary teams

Creative Examples (personal)
★ your contribution to a team effort
★ a list of successful teams you have been on
★ a personal success that was due to team effort
★ a time when you transcended yourself while part of a team
★ an experience when you used reflective listening

Teacher's Personal Reflection Log

A FEW OF MY FAVORITE INTELLIGENCE THINGS

I have the following thoughts/insights about the A Few of My Favorite Intelligence Things strategy:

I feel that the A Few of My Favorite Intelligence Things strategy can help me in my teaching in the following ways:

As a learning process, the A Few of My Favorite Intelligence Things strategy includes the following benefits for my students:

I have the following specific ideas for using the A Few of My Favorite Intelligence Things strategy in my classroom in the near future:

I think the A Few of My Favorite Intelligence Things strategy can be used beyond the classroom and school in the following ways:

Seven Pathways of Learning © 1994 Zephyr Press, Tucson, Arizona

NOTES TO PARENTS

The Reflective Level of the Seven Ways of Knowing

The purpose of the reflective level of teaching and learning about the seven ways of knowing is to help students approach the task of daily living using more of their multiple intelligences. This approach involves encouraging children to use all of their intelligence capabilities to become more effective in dealing with the issues, challenges, and problems they face, and will face, in everyday life. Students should learn to approach these aspects of their lives on multiple levels, with a variety of problem-solving methods that use different intelligences. I am concerned with having students integrate the intelligences into their repertoire for living. I am also concerned that children learn to apply the intelligences appropriately to situations they encounter in the so-called real world, the world beyond the classroom. The goal at this level is for the intelligences to become a regular part of students' cognitive, affective, and sensory coping with life.

In the learning process, we often learn something in one situation but fail to see how it applies in another. When I was a child I took more than nine years of music lessons to learn to play the piano and bassoon. I enjoyed this learning very much, but for the most part saw little application of it beyond my own enjoyment. I was barely making my way through a required algebra course in college, however, when my professor, a very skilled musician, one day showed me how math and music are alike: "In math" he said, "you learn numbers. In music you learn notes. They are both abstract and symbolic representations of something else (quantity on the one hand and tones on the other). In math you learn certain operations and processes that link numbers in different meaningful patterns. In music you learn to link the notes in certain specified ways to make a tune." He also pointed out that math has its special jargon—ratio, square root, proportion, and so on—that tells you what to do with a set of numbers. Music has its special jargon, as well—clef signs, flats, sharps, rhythm, and so on—that tells you what to do with a set of notes. Suddenly, I had a new way to approach math using something in which I was confident and that I liked. I didn't get an A in the class, but my performance did improve, as did my enjoyment of the class.

In working with the reflective level of the intelligences, we are trying to help children make connections between their intelligence skills or capacities and other parts of their lives. I believe this connection can be made very quickly in the classroom, for there, an intelligence skill learned in one subject area can quite easily be bridged or transferred into another subject area. Helping students take their intelligences beyond the classroom into everyday life, however, is a task that no one can do as well as a parent. The following suggestions are intended to give you a starting place to help your children make the connections between their seven ways of knowing and their daily lives. Once you have tried a few of these suggestions, I'm sure you will begin to come up with many, much better ideas on your own.

Activities to Support the Reflective Use of the Intelligences

Verbal/Linguistic

★ When your child has a firm opinion about something, ask her to create and deliver a convincing argument for the opposite position.

★ List things in which your child shows special interest or things that he enjoys. Have your child create an explanation, the "why" for each item on the list, and tell it others.

★ Develop your child's "debating skills" (that is, the ability to defend her thinking) by playing the devil's advocate and forcing her to explain her position.

★ Work with your child to help him understand such things as cartoons or comic strips, puns, and punch lines to jokes.

Visual/Spatial

★ When your child is experiencing some problem or difficulty have her draw pictures or images of the difficulty and explain what the pictures mean; explore solutions by adding other images to the pictures.

★ Teach your child to use his active imagination to plan or deal with a challenge (for example, he imagines the results or consequences of certain actions).

★ Teach your child the art of mental rehearsal for an important task she has to perform; in the mind's eye, she pictures the task going perfectly.

★ Help your child learn various techniques to keep from getting lost in new places: reading maps, sighting landmarks, and so on.

Logical/Mathematical

★ Help your child become aware of various behavior patterns—ones that work well for him and ones that often trip him up.

★ Work with your child to establish certain healthy routines or schedules in daily life, including eating healthfully.

★ Teach your child how to set goals and then to work backward from a goal to develop the logical steps that will help her achieve that goal.

★ Work with your child to help him learn such applied intelligence skills as balancing a checkbook, making a calendar, planning a party, and so on.

Bodily/Kinesthetic

★ Help your child learn how to act out her emotions about things happening in her life.

★ Play "Body Language Jeopardy": one person does a gesture or posture and the other tells what it means and the feelings it conveys. Talk about the use of appropriate body language in everyday communication.

★ Work with your child to develop "multi-tracking" skills he will need in daily life. Multi-tracking is the ability to do several things at the same time, such as cooking, listening to the news, and watching the baby.

★ Practice dramatic enactment of an idea or opinion your child has about something.

★ Show your child appropriate hand gestures or body movements to go along with a story as you read it.

Seven Pathways of Learning © 1994 Zephyr Press, Tucson, Arizona

Activities to Support the Reflective Use of the Intelligences

Musical/Rhythmic

★ Work with your child to create ridiculous songs about problems or issues she is facing; also make up verses about possible solutions.

★ Help your child learn how to use different kinds of music to change mood, such as music to relax in stressful situations and music to improve performance in various tasks (music that helps a person achieve a steady rhythm in typing is one example).

★ Brainstorm different kinds of music your child can play to help him with different tasks, such as cleaning a room, doing homework, exercising, and so on.

★ Help your child learn to listen to the sounds in different situations and learn what they tell her: the sound of the traffic, sounds from nature, the sounds other people make, and so on.

Intrapersonal

★ Have your child start keeping a diary or journal in which he writes or draws about things that happened during the day, including the emotions he felt.

★ Teach your child how to have an imaginary conversation with someone or something that she found upsetting during the day, speaking about the feelings she experienced and how to resolve the feelings.

★ Help your child learn to project himself into a future situation and to anticipate how he will handle difficulties and challenges that arise.

★ Work with your child on different techniques for building positive self-esteem and esteem for others: affirmation exercises, writing paragraphs entitled "What's Right with Me," creating personal symbols of possibility, and so on.

Interpersonal

★ Have the whole family give input on a personal decision a member is facing; then prioritize the different suggestions together.

★ Experiment with a family council in which individuals are allowed to air complaints, share difficulties, celebrate successes, plan, and share ideas.

★ Teach your child to do reflective listening, which is listening and paraphrasing what has been said, asking the other person about his or her feelings, making observations about body language, and so on.

★ Give your child a list of interpersonal relationship skills and target time to work on developing one skill per week as a family.

5

The Multiple Intelligence School

A FUTURE SCENARIO

For a moment pretend that you have mysteriously shown up in a culture that has no education system and that you have been assigned to invent, from scratch, such a system. What would you create? What would the curriculum be? Whom would you select as teachers? Where would the teaching or learning take place?

In Howard Gardner's book *The Unschooled Mind: How Children Think and How Schools Should Teach,* he presents a compelling and intriguing new image of the educational process. I suggest you read the following quotation from this book, and after each section, close your eyes and try to visualize the scene the words suggest. You might even have some paper and markers nearby so you can sketch what you see with your mind's eye.[6]

6. The quotation is from Gardner 1991; the format and suggestions for visualization and drawing exercises are mine.

Imagine an education environment in which youngsters at the age of 7 or 8, in addition to—or perhaps instead of—attending a formal school, have the opportunity to enroll in a children's museum, a science museum, or some kind of discovery center or exploratorium. As part of this educational scene, adults are present who actually practice the disciplines or crafts represented by the various exhibitions.

Pause, visualize, and draw.

During the course of their school, youngsters enter into separate apprenticeships with a number of these adults. Each apprentice group consists of students of different ages and varying degrees of expertise in the domain or discipline. As part of the apprenticeship, the child is drawn into the use of various disciplines. . . . The student's apprenticeships deliberately encompass a range of pursuits, including artistic activities, activities requiring exercise and dexterity, and activities of a more scholarly bent.

Pause, visualize, and draw.

Most of the learning and most of the assessment are done cooperatively; that is, students work together on projects that typically require a team of people having different degrees of and complementary kinds of skills. Thus, the team assembling the bicycle might consist of half a dozen youngsters, whose tasks range from locating and fitting together parts to inspecting the newly assembled systems to revising a manual or preparing advertising copy.

Pause, visualize, and draw.

The assessment of learning also assumes a variety of forms, ranging from the student's monitoring her own learning by keeping a journal to "the test of the street"—does the bicycle actually operate satisfactorily, and does it find any buyers?

Pause, visualize, and draw.

Because the older people on the team, or "coaches," are skilled professionals who see themselves as training future members of their trade, the reasons for activities are clear, the standards are high, and satisfaction flows from a job well done.

Pause, visualize, and draw.

And because the students are enrolled from the first in a meaningful and challenging activity, they come to feel a genuine stake in the outcome of their (and their peers') efforts.

Pause, visualize, and draw.

Seven Pathways of Learning © 1994 Zephyr Press, Tucson, Arizona

In another publication Gardner (1990) suggests that in a multiple intelligence school students might spend half of each day studying the traditional subjects but in very nontraditional ways. Students would master the content of particular subject areas by creating a variety of projects, experiments, and exhibitions. For example, they might be given problems to solve that people in the real world face, such as designing a new playground, investigating conflicting reports about an event in the community, or creating advertisements for a school function. They would spend the second half of the day out in the community exploring their classroom learning in context: by visiting museums and discovery centers, and by getting involved in apprenticeships or by bringing the community into the classroom.

If we are talking about implementing the theory of multiple intelligences fully in our schools, we are talking about an educational system that is radically different from what we currently have. In this final chapter I will explore some implications of using the theory and practice behind multiple intelligences for restructuring schools. I believe that something similar to what I am suggesting is a vital part of the reinvention of the educational paradigm for the 90s and beyond. In fact I would even suggest there may be no greater tool for transforming education today than restructuring our schools so they are places that teach students how to be more intelligent beings!

From the perspective of multiple intelligence theory, *the paramount restructuring goal is to promote the fullest possible intellectual development of our students.* I believe that there are four restructuring areas with which we need to be concerned, each of which promotes our students' full intellectual development.

OVERVIEW

Restructuring the Curriculum
(Teaching FOR Multiple Intelligences)

We promote the full intellectual development of our students when we explicitly teach them the core skills of each of the seven intelligences. This area involve restructuring the curriculum. We must evaluate the curricula of our various educational institutions to ensure that within them students are learning the specific sets of core skills necessary to be able to utilize the full spectrum of these students' intellectual capabilities. This analysis must take us far beyond but include verbal/linguistic and logical/mathematical skills, which are the current biases of our Western educational systems.

Restructuring Instruction
(Teaching WITH Multiple Intelligences)

We promote the full intellectual development of our students when we present every lesson using multiple teaching and learning strategies and encourage students to process information using all seven intelligences. This area involves restructuring instructional technologies and practices. We must reconsider our own teaching methodologies and techniques to ensure that we teach everything in multiple ways; not all students know, understand, perceive, and learn in the same way. Instruction must be more individualized and tailored to students' varying intelligence strengths and weaknesses.

Restructuring the Learning Process
(Teaching ABOUT Multiple Intelligences)

We promote the full intellectual development of our students when we help them learn about their intelligences and how those intelligences function, and when we work with parents to help them understand the seven ways of knowing. This area involves reinventing the learning process itself. We must find the time to provide students with opportunities to learn about their own multiple intelligence capacities. Students need occasions to explore and develop their various ways of knowing, both within the traditional school setting and in their lives beyond the classroom.

Restructuring Assessment
(Multimodal Testing through the Multiple Intelligences)

We promote the full intellectual development of our students when we provide intelligence-fair testing to determine relative strengths and weakness in all intelligence areas and when we use a wide variety of testing modes to evaluate students' academic progress. This area involves restructuring the way we assess students at all levels. We must create appropriate and authentic means for examining students' various intelligence capabilities as well as students' learning in specific subjects and content areas. We need to be teaching students to transfer intelligence across the curriculum and into their lives beyond the school situation.

Seven Pathways of Learning © 1994 Zephyr Press, Tucson, Arizona

RESTRUCTURING THE CURRICULUM

Please do the survey on page 194 before reading this section.

Multiple Intelligence Capacities or Skills

In some ways we can view our intelligence capacities as the building blocks necessary to utilize the various ways of knowing fully and effectively. Without these building blocks, the full potential of a particular intelligence is not available to us. Think for a moment what it would be like to try to teach mathematical problem solving if your students didn't have the skills of number sequencing, basic calculation, and recognition of patterns? What would happen if you tried to teach English to students who did not possess the skills of reading, writing, verbal communication, and humor? The logical/mathematical and the verbal/linguistic ways of knowing would simply not be fully available to those students.

We educators may be more familiar with the background capacities students must master in order to be skillful in the language arts and math, but we may not realize that the same kind of careful skill instruction is needed to help students develop capacities in each of the intelligence areas; that is, if we want students to be able to use the full spectrum of their intellectual capabilities, they must be taught explicitly the skills of each intelligence, in the same manner as we currently teach students the ABCs, counting, vocabulary, arithmetic operations, and so on. If we want them to develop their visual/spatial capacities, for example, we must explicitly teach them such things as how to use their active imaginations, how to make graphic representations, how to manipulate images, and how to find their way around a given location. If we want them to develop their musical/rhythmic intelligence, we must teach them how to recognize the meaning of various sounds and tones, how to produce meaningful tones themselves, and how to carry a tune.

The Multiple Intelligence Capacities Inventory Wheel on page 21 suggests a categorization of different capacities, potentials, and skills that are necessary if one is to use the seven intelligences effectively. Howard Gardner sometimes refers to these as "sub-intelligences." They represent various sets of core capacities inherent in human beings' central nervous system. We can consciously develop these core capacities and improve them through various kinds of exercises and practices. (See *Seven Ways of Knowing* if you are not familiar with these).

It is crucial that we teach all of these capacities to all students, and the capacities must be integrated or embedded in the curriculum itself. We must not consider development of multiple intelligence capacities an "add on." I suggest that we need to restructure our curriculum guides so that, as we present the curriculum, we are developing our students' multiple intelligences. In doing so we will be helping students actualize their full intellectual potential.

Restructuring the Curriculum
What skills and capacities should we be teaching?

Teaching FOR Multiple Intelligences Survey

Place an "X" in the box by any item that you feel is true of your regular teaching approaches.

☐ **My classroom provides students with a sensory-rich learning environment (i.e., opportunities to see, touch, smell, taste, hear, and think about each lesson).**

☐ **My students are aware of the seven ways of knowing.**

☐ **I teach my students how to access or trigger the seven intelligences within their own brain/mind/body systems.**

☐ **I am aware of the capacities my students need beyond the traditional three Rs and I am teaching them these skills.**

☐ **I provide opportunities for students to practice using different ways of knowing and learning that go beyond the traditional verbal/linguistic and logical/mathematical modes.**

☐ **I am aware of and use various practices for helping my students amplify the full spectrum of their intellectual capabilities.**

What I am suggesting has nothing whatsoever to do with what our culture usually calls "talent," whether it be musical, artistic, mathematical, dramatic, literary, or what have you. We all possess all seven ways of knowing, and likely many more than seven! We can use these ways to acquire knowledge, understand our world, improve our ability to solve problems, create, and meet the challenges we face in our daily lives whether or not the larger culture would call us talented.

Developmental Pathways of the Intelligences

How do the intelligences develop? When do the different capacities and skills normally appear in human development? What can we do to assist and catalyze the development of the full spectrum of intellectual capabilities?

We are most likely familiar with Jean Piaget's brilliant picture of the journey of children's cognitive development. We must remember, however, that Piaget's work dealt mostly with the development of logical/mathematical intelligence. One of the keys for launching a true transformation of the curriculum is to flesh out Piaget-type models to include pictures of how each of the intelligences evolves and matures, including the necessary inputs and catalysts along the way.

In the second edition of *Seven Ways of Knowing* (1991) I outline four stages that represent the general evolution of an intelligence:

1. The first and earliest stage is the *acquisition of the basic capacities and skills* for each intelligence. This could also be called the "novice stage." This stage is more or less guaranteed for the general population both by our biological makeup and by the various socialization processes of our cultures. These capacities are generally learned almost by osmosis, from family, environment, and other factors that are part of our early childhood experiences.

2. The second broad stage of development involves an *expanded and more complex development of all intelligence skills*. This stage begins most often when children start their formal education. They learn to expand their basic skills and to use them in various problem-solving tasks. They also learn the "language" and "symbol systems" for each of the intelligences.

3. The third stage involves *the development of higher-order intelligence capacities* and generally begins with a person's secondary schooling. During this period of intellectual development students learn to integrate the seven intelligences into their normal daily functioning, to employ different ways of knowing to help attain personal goals, and to use many modes to solve problems and meet challenges.

4. The final developmental stage is often directly related to one's *vocational or avocational pursuits*. This level usually represents mastery as

well as the conscious use of one's intelligences to be of service to the larger social order.

In public education we have often relied on our so-called fine arts programs and "extracurricular" activities to teach the skills and develop the intelligence capacities that go beyond the so-called academic subjects, which tend to emphasize the development of verbal/linguistic and logical/mathematical skills. I believe we must hang onto and expand our fine arts programs, for it is often these so-called extra parts of the curriculum that teach students the basic capacities and skills they need to use the different ways of knowing. Unfortunately, these curricular offerings are the first to be cut when school districts face necessary budget cuts. In light of this, I strongly advocate that every classroom teacher must find and teach the "fine arts" components that are part of every subject area. Or even better, let us thoroughly integrate the fine arts and academic curricula; it's time to take the "extra" out of "extracurricular" and make it all curricular!

Curriculum Analysis Exercise*

How Intelligent Is Your Curriculum?

In this exercise you will have an opportunity to take a new look at the curriculum you are teaching and to analyze it in terms of the multiple intelligences. You will be using the Multiple Intelligence Capacities Inventory presented earlier in this book (p. 21).

1. Make a copy of the Curriculum Analysis work sheet on page 197.
2. Review the capacities related to the intelligences on the Capacities Inventory Wheel (p. 21). After reviewing each, make notes of the impressions you have of your curriculum on the Curriculum Analysis Work Sheet:

    • In the first column, note specific areas (for example, academic subjects, after-school activities, special classes, and so on) in which students are explicitly taught the capacities or skills of the various intelligences.
    • In the second column, rank the intelligences from strongest to weakest in terms of the numbers of skills that are part of what is taught in your school.

3. Now spend some time creating a new curricular vision—a vision in which the fine arts are integrated completely into the so-called academic subjects and one in which the extracurricular is curricular:

    • In the third column, list three to five areas in which you see fresh, new opportunities to teach students the skills of the seven intelligences.

*Permission to reprint Curriculum Analysis Exercise granted by Phi Delta Kappa.

Curriculum Analysis Work Sheet

	WHERE CURRENTLY TAUGHT	RANK	NEW OPPORTUNITIES TO TEACH	RANK	TOTAL
Verbal/Linguistic intelligence					
Logical/Mathematical intelligence					
Visual/Spatial intelligence					
Bodily/Kinesthetic intelligence					
Musical/Rhythmic intelligence					
Intrapersonal intelligence					
Interpersonal intelligence					

- In the fourth column, rank the intelligences based on these new ideas. Compare this new ranking with your previous one. What differences do you notice?

4. Now total the two rankings, the skills that are currently being taught and the new opportunities for teaching the skills, in the fifth column.

   - Write three to five statements about what these lists reveal about the directions curriculum reform needs to take in your school or district.
   - Brainstorm a list of strategic steps you can take *in your current position* to begin the process of restructuring curriculum. Include both immediate and long-range strategies.

RESTRUCTURING INSTRUCTION

Please do the survey on page 199 before reading this section.

Staging Multiple Intelligence Lessons

Generally speaking, there are four stages to teaching with multiple intelligences. These stages make teaching compatible with how the brain actually works. When we teach in brain-compatible ways, we get better thinking and information processing, higher levels of creativity, greater transfer of learning, raised self-esteem, and higher degrees of motivation from our students. Dr. Jean Houston (1980) at the Foundation for Mind Research has researched the idea of multiperceptual learning and states the following:

> We are as different from each other as snowflakes; and each of us has, especially in childhood, a special penchant for different ways of exploring our world. In order to preserve the genius and developmental potential of childhood, one must quite simply give the universe back to the child, in as rich and dramatic a form as possible.
>
> *Multiperceptual learning,* we have found, is a key to this gifting. In school curricula and programs . . . the child is taught to think in images as well as in words, to learn spelling or even arithmetic in rhythmic patterns, to think with his whole body— in short, to *learn school subjects, and more, from a much larger spectrum of sensory and cognitive possibilities.* (emphasis mine)

Art Costa (1991) supports this multimodal concept. He notes that there are fourteen characteristics of intelligent behavior. "Using all the senses" is one of these ways of knowing and being intelligent:

> Language, culture, and physical learning are all derived from our senses. To know a wine it must be drunk; to know a role it must be acted; to know a game it must be played; to know a dance it must be moved; to know a goal it must be

Restructuring Instruction
How can we help more kids succeed more of the time?

Teaching WITH Multiple Intelligences Survey

Place an "X" in the box by any item that you feel is true of
your regular teaching approaches.

☐ **My daily classroom teaching integrates multiple intelligence
strategies and tools into lessons that deal with the different
subject areas.**

☐ **I encourage and require my students to process information
from a lesson using all seven ways of knowing.**

☐ **In my lesson planning, I think through how to teach every
lesson using all seven intelligences even if I don't use all
seven in each lesson.**

☐ **I have a system that tracks my teaching to make sure that I
use all seven intelligences every week and that I am teaching
in an intelligence-balanced manner.**

☐ **I am experimenting with new forms of authentic academic
assessment that take into account the seven intelligences.**

☐ **I know how to stage lessons so that they are compatible with
the neurobiological functioning of the different intelligences.**

Seven Pathways of Learning © 1994 Zephyr Press, Tucson, Arizona

envisioned. Those whose sensory pathways are open and alert absorb more information from the environment than those whose pathways are oblivious to sensory stimuli.

We can observe students using their senses when they touch objects in their environment, when they request that a story or rhyme be read again and again, or when they act out roles. Often, what they say tells us that their senses are engaged: "Let me see, let me see . . . " "I want to feel it . . ." "Let me try it . . . " "Let me hold it . . . "

As children mature, we can observe that they conceive and express many ways of solving problems by the use of the senses. . . . Their expressions use a range and variety of sensory words: "I feel like . . . " "It touches me," "I hear your ideas," "It leaves a bad taste in my mouth," "Get the picture?"

The diagram on page 201 is from *Seven Ways of Teaching* and is a model for staging intelligence-compatible lessons.

Stage 1: Awakening the Intelligences[7]

Since each intelligence has a neurological and biological base, we can consciously activate the intelligences by performing certain brain/mind exercises, such as those suggested in the first chapter. The goal of the awakening stage in a lesson is to stimulate specific areas of the brain/mind/body system to wake up certain intelligence capacities that may be dormant.

For example, if you want to activate visual/spatial capacities, the mere act of passing out colored markers, paints, crayons, or clay will often do the job. If you want to trigger bodily/kinesthetic capacities in a lesson, any kind of physical movement, including dance, role-playing, and body gestures, will suffice. In many ways the specific media of an intelligence are in and of themselves a message to latent intelligence capacities in the brain to "wake up and get ready for action!"

In this awakening stage we are concerned first with becoming aware that we do in fact possess multiple ways of knowing and learning, and second with learning techniques for stimulating the different intelligences within the brain/mind/body system.

Stage 2: Amplifying the Intelligences

We can enhance, strengthen, and improve each of the intelligences. In some ways intelligence capacities are like any skill we possess: the more we practice the better we become. The goal of the amplifying stage is to focus on developing or strengthening intelligence areas in which one is uncomfortable or weak.

To improve students' interpersonal intelligence capacities, for example, you must teach them certain relational skills, such as listening,

7. The following description is adapted with permission from the PDK Fastback series.

What Does It Take to Teach Intelligence?[8]

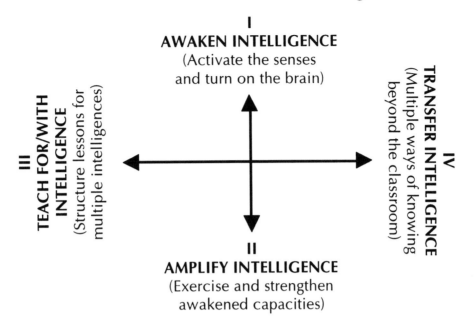

Stage I
AWAKEN INTELLIGENCE

Since each intelligence is related to the five senses, we can activate or trigger the intelligences. This stage involves exercises and activities that use the following bases: sight, sound, taste, touch, smell, and speech; communication with others; and the inner senses, such as intuition, metacognition, and spiritual insight.

Stage II
AMPLIFY INTELLIGENCE

This stage involves practices for expanding, deepening, and nurturing an awakened or activated intelligence. As with any skill, not only can we awaken our intelligence skills but we can improve and strengthen them if we use them regularly. And, like any skill, they will go back to sleep or atrophy if we do not use them.

Stage III
TEACH FOR/WITH INTELLIGENCE

This stage involves learning how to use, to trust, and to interpret a given intelligence through knowing, learning, and understanding tasks. I use classroom lessons that emphasize and use different intelligences to teach with intelligence.

Stage IV
TRANSFER INTELLIGENCE

This stage integrates an intelligence into daily living, and we learn to apply it appropriately to solving problems and meeting the challenges we face in the "real world." The goal of this stage is for the intelligence to become a regular part of our cognitive, affective, and sensory lives.

8. Adapted from Lazear, David. *Seven Ways of Teaching.* Palatine, Ill.: Skylight, 1991.

encouraging others, reaching consensus, and so on, and then give them opportunities to practice the skills. If you want to amplify musical/rhythmic capacities, work to help students develop recognition of different sounds, practice matching a rhythmic pattern or tune produced by another, or learn to express emotions through sound alone.

In this stage, we are concerned with learning how particular intelligences function and how to work to improve them. We must understand the different capacities and skills of the intelligences, how to access them, and how to use these capacities or skills effectively.

Stage 3: Teaching with the Intelligences

Once an intelligence has been awakened and we have learned to strengthen our skills in using it, we can employ the intelligence to gain specific information or acquire knowledge. The goal of the teaching stage is to present content-based lessons that apply different ways of knowing to the teaching and learning process required to master academic material.

One can learn vocabulary words with the body, for example, physically "em- bodying" the words' meanings (bodily/kinesthetic). You can teach the parts of a tree by having students make clay models of trees that illustrate the different parts (visual/spatial). Students can learn the states and capitals by creating a rap or song with the information (musical/rhythmic).

We must remember that about 95 percent of the material we have to teach as educators comes prepackaged in a verbal/linguistic or a logical/mathematical form. In planning lessons, however, we must not be bound by this packaging. We can and should design lessons that emphasize all seven ways of knowing.

Stage 4: Transferring the Intelligence

The final stage is to integrate the intelligences into one's daily living. This integration includes learning how to apply the intelligences to solve problems and to meet challenges faced in the world beyond the classroom. The goal of the transfer stage is to make the intelligences a regular part of one's cognitive, affective, and sensory repertoire for living.

Once students have learned how to succeed in a cooperative learning situation, for example, they can transfer the same skills to their family to improve the relating and cooperation among family members (interpersonal). Or they can use reflective logs beyond the classroom by keeping daily or weekly journals to reflect on their lives (intrapersonal).

We must teach our students how to use all of the intelligences to improve their effectiveness in dealing with the issues and challenges they encounter in the task of daily living. This task is primarily one of learning strategies for approaching all aspects of living on multiple levels, with a variety of problem-solving methods that engage the full spectrum of the intelligences.

You may be asking, "What about time? I've got so much to cover and only a limited time in which to do it!" Art Costa (1991) has observed that one of the effects contemporary cognitive research has had on today's educational systems is that taking precious classroom time to teach students how to think and learn is gaining wider acceptance:

> As a result of this wider acceptance, thinking skills are not being viewed as mere additions to an already over-crowded, time-squeezed, cemeterial compendium of scopes and sequences. Rather teachers are finding comfort, agreement, and rededication in some common goals—that process is as important as product; that thoughtful and reflective thinking (rather than coverage) is acceptable once again; and that students' production of knowledge is as important as their reproduction of knowledge.

In the staff development workshops I conduct, the question, "How can we teach the way you're suggesting when we have so much we have to cover in a normal school day?" is often raised. In one such training, a high school history teacher asked the group if they knew Webster's definition of the verb "to cover." He informed us that its primary meaning is "to hide from view." He then posed the provocative question, "Is this in fact what we're doing when we are so preoccupied with covering the curriculum? Maybe," he suggested, "we should be uncovering the curriculum for our students. Maybe this is a far greater service to them!"

His statements apply beautifully to teaching with multiple intelligences. The good news about teaching with multiple intelligences is that doing so is not an additional task to what we have to teach anyway. I am not suggesting that we should be teaching more "stuff" in an already over-stuffed curriculum. But I am suggesting that we teach the old stuff in a radically new way!

When we work with the intelligences in daily lessons, the key is first to trigger the seven ways of knowing within the class, which gives students an opportunity to practice using the full spectrum of their intelligences, and then to move into the lesson at hand utilizing the intelligence(s) that have been awakened and the skills that students have practiced. The Multiple Intelligences Toolbox in chapter 3 is a quick lesson planning device to help you easily move anything you have to teach to multiple levels of knowing, learning, and understanding. One very effective use of the Multiple Intelligences Toolbox is as a brainstorm aid for exploring the multiple intelligence possibilities for a given lesson. Simply select one tool from each intelligence and then plan the lesson around those tools. (If you are unfamiliar with the "MI toolbox" and how to use it in detailed lesson planning, see Lazear 1991b).

RESTRUCTURING THE LEARNING PROCESS

Please do the survey on page 205 before reading this section.

Reinventing the Learning Process: Meta-Intelligence as Transformational Process

In some ways, the restructuring or reinventing of the learning process integrates all that I have suggested in the previous parts of this chapter. I have called this area "meta-intelligence." As you have seen in this book, it is the most complex and probably the most holistic aspect of working with the multiple intelligences. Teaching *about* multiple intelligences assumes and encompasses teaching *for* and *with* the intelligences! The chart on page 206 illustrates this idea.

Brain-Based Teaching and Learning

The tacit level involves learning how to access or trigger the different intelligences in the brain/mind/body system. Generally this awakening can be achieved through exercises, games, puzzles, and the like that are designed to stimulate different areas of the brain.

The aware level involves an understanding of the modalities by which each intelligence processes information. Each intelligence has its own language and method of processing. For example, the language and processing modality of visual/spatial intelligence is colors, textures, shapes, images, patterns, designs, and pictures. Visual/spatial intelligence simply does not understand such things as alphabets, words, sentences, paragraphs, and the like.

The strategic level involves the ability to call upon the seven ways of knowing to assist you in a variety of situations. For example, putting something you're having a hard time remembering to music, expressing or changing feelings through physical exercise or movement, or drawing diagrams to help someone understand an idea.

The reflective level involves knowing how to bring a number of intelligences to bear on a single issue or topic. This level requires knowledge of how each intelligence works and what it takes to access its wisdom and input quickly.

Intelligence Enhancement and Expansion

The tacit level involves knowledge of practices for strengthening and improving the intelligences. Through the disciplined exercising of different intelligence skills, one can strengthen those skills by using all seven ways of knowing. Remember, "practice makes perfect."

Restructuring the Learning Process
How can we help kids reach their full learning potential in school?

Teaching ABOUT Multiple Intelligences Survey

Place an "X" in the box by any item that you feel is true of your regular teaching approaches.

☐ **My students are aware of and know how to use different tools to access their own multiple ways of knowing, understanding, and learning in a lesson.**

☐ **I am working to create intelligence profiles for each of my students so that I am aware of their strengths and weaknesses in each of the intelligences.**

☐ **In my weekly lesson planning, I include time for students to be "meta-intelligent" (i.e., to think about, evaluate, understand, and work on improving all seven ways of knowing).**

☐ **I am providing information and training that teaches parents how to deal with multiple intelligences and how to use and nurture the intelligences at home.**

☐ **I have a plan for moving my students through the different meta-intelligence levels, from the tacit to the reflective.**

☐ **My students keep an intelligence portfolio in which they reflect on what they are learning about themselves and their own intelligence potentials and keep ideas they have for applying the seven ways of knowing to life beyond the school.**

Dynamics of Meta-Intelligence

Brain-Based Teaching and Learning (teaching FOR multiple intelligences)	**Intelligence Enhancement and Expansion** (teaching WITH multiple intelligences)	**Appropriate Transfer and Application** (teaching ABOUT multiple intelligences)
• **knowledge of the various intelligence triggers** (tacit level) • **understanding the language of each intelligence** (aware level) • **ability to access the intelligences in varying situations** (strategic level) • **knowing how to switch between the intelligences** (reflective level)	• **knowledge of intelligence-amplifying practices** (tacit level) • **understanding the symbol systems of the intelligences** (aware level) • **ability to interpret or process intelligence data accurately** (strategic level) • **knowing one's own intelligence strengths or weaknesses** (reflective level)	• **knowledge of different meta-intelligence levels** (tacit level) • **understanding intelligence translation processes** (aware level) • **ability to utilize the intelligences to solve problems** (strategic level) • **knowing when to use which of the seven intelligences** (reflective level)

Seven Pathways of Learning © 1994 Zephyr Press, Tucson, Arizona

The aware level involves understanding what Gardner calls "notational systems." Each intelligence has its own symbol system for communication. For example, the symbol system for musical/rhythmic intelligence is notes arranged on a staff that represent a tune to be played at a specified rhythm and pitch. This symbolic or notational dimension of the intelligences is what allows their wisdom and knowledge to be transmitted.

The strategic level involves the accurate interpretation of various kinds of information generated by the intelligences. Developing the ability to read and understand that information is a matter of learning to recognize certain patterns of communication, to interpret and appreciate the meaning of nonverbal data, and to process traditional information in multiple, nontraditional ways.

The reflective level involves the skills of accurately evaluating one's own intelligence strengths and weakness. It also involves knowledge of such things as exercises or practices for improving weaker intelligences and knowing how to use a stronger way of knowing to train a weaker one.

Appropriate Transfer and Application

The tacit level involves knowledge of the various stages of meta-intelligence (or teaching about the intelligences) and skill in helping others learn about, explore, and come to understand something of their own multiple ways of knowing, understanding, perceiving, and learning.

The aware level involves an understanding of the "translation process" involved in working seriously with multiple intelligences; namely, translating verbal/linguistic information into other modalities. For example, you can translate geometric formulas into a dance, vocabulary words into clay sculptures, or the parts of a cell into a rap.

The strategic level involves the ability to use all seven intelligences to solve problems and to deal with challenges faced in the task of living. This ability involves skill in problem analysis and an understanding of the creative process, as well as how to tap into higher levels of creativity and thinking through the intelligences.

The reflective level involves knowing when to use which intelligence to deal with what situation. At this level, the seven ways of knowing are no longer something external to one's being; they have become fully integrated and are a part of the "equipment" one uses in the task of effective living.

RESTRUCTURING ASSESSMENT

Please do the survey on page 209 before reading this section.

The Assessment Conundrum: "To Test, or Not to Test? That Is the Question!"

A major concern in teaching about multiple intelligences is how to assess students' intelligence capacities so we can help them be better learners, and how to evaluate their academic progress. To address the first concern, we must devise ways to help us recognize and understand students' relative strengths and weaknesses in the seven intelligence areas. This assessment is obviously important, as current research indicates that intelligence is not fixed or static as we once thought. In fact, intelligence appears to be a dynamic, continually evolving process.

This information is important from at least three perspectives:

1. We can help students develop a fuller spectrum of intellectual abilities to use in the classroom, and in their lives beyond the classroom
2. We can find new strategies for helping students use their stronger intelligences to succeed in school.
3. We can use a student's strength in one intelligence to strengthen a weakness in another.

Howard Gardner suggests that when we try to assess the intelligences of students, we need a profile of their intelligences, not decontextualized scores. The process of intelligence assessment is somewhat akin to putting together a jigsaw puzzle: no single piece of the puzzle gives you the whole picture; only when all the pieces are together do you see the whole. The job is to figure out what makes each student tick intellectually, that is, to figure out how students best know, understand, perceive, and learn. Gardner believes that with about ten hours of careful observation of students involved in various activities and learning tasks, we can get a fairly accurate intelligence profile of our students. We can use this information to help them master their studies and deal with everyday problems and challenges, and to give them vocational guidance counseling later in their educational journey.

The second area of authentic assessment involves employing multiple intelligence ways to evaluate students' academic progress. My concern here again is to gain a holistic picture of what students know—beyond what can be demonstrated on the typical paper-and-pencil test. We can rest assured that even the best students know more than they can adequately show on most of the tests we give. I am not suggesting that there is something wrong with paper-and-pencil tests, as long as we keep them in their proper place and don't try to make them the sole indicator of what a student knows or has learned in a given lesson or unit.

Restructuring Assessment

How can we use assessment to give us an
authentic picture of the whole child?

Authentic Assessment Survey

Place an "X" in the box by any item that you feel is true
of your regular teaching approaches.

☐ **I allow and encourage my students to demonstrate what they have learned using a wide variety of methods, including, but not limited to, paper-and-pencil methods.**

☐ **I know how to help students transfer their unique ways of knowing and learning to perform successfully on required, standardized tests.**

☐ **I continually watch my students as they are involved in various learning tasks or activities to gain a fuller picture of their intelligence profiles.**

☐ **I am experimenting with the creation and testing of intelligence-fair ways to assess students' academic progress.**

☐ **I am experimenting with a new kind of whole child report card that not only evaluates academic skills, but also provides feedback on the different intelligence skills and capacities the student has mastered.**

☐ **I provide administrators and my fellow teachers with the most up-to-date information about multiple intelligence research, including inviting them to observe applications I am using in my classroom.**

Project Spectrum

Project Spectrum is an innovative research effort focused on assessment in early childhood. It is based on Gardner's work. In the February 1991 edition of *Education Leadership* Mara Krechevsky summarizes five key factors of Spectrum's assessment system. I believe that these hold clues for all levels and may help us solve the assessment conundrum:

1. **Blurring the lines between curriculum and assessment.** This means that teachers gather information from their careful observation of students who are involved in a wide variety of learning tasks and activities. No single paper-and-pencil test (nor any other single test) should be used to determine what a student knows or has learned in a particular unit. We should be assessing how our students are doing all of the time, not just on traditional exams, and we should be doing so by using a wide variety of forms such as student-created portfolios, reflective logs and journals, videos of students demonstrating something they have learned, and so on.

2. **Embedding assessment in meaningful, real-world activities.** Rather than focusing on skills that are meaningful in the school context only, Project Spectrum suggests that assessment be focused on abilities and skills relevant to achieving rewarding roles later in life. In other words, what we teach and how we test should be grounded in the real world outside of the school setting. Nowhere in real life does anyone ever encounter the typical standardized test that calls for the simple regurgitation of memorized facts and information (except perhaps when applying for a driver's license). Life is about application! It is about doing something with what we know! Instead of having students spend hours memorizing the rules of grammar, why not have them create a class newspaper and try to instill in them the love of communicating their ideas to others? Or have them create something that requires the meaningful use of math facts, processes, and operations?

3. **Using measures that are "intelligence fair."** Most standardized tests view students' learning only through the glasses of verbal/linguistic and logical/mathematical abilities. Why not allow students to use a wide range of media to demonstrate what they know and have learned? Experiment with allowing students to use nontraditional ways that go beyond the verbal/linguistic and logical/mathematical to demonstrate their knowledge of a topic. For example, on a math test, you might involve bodily/kinesthetic knowing by couching it in terms of body movement itself, including gestures, physical action, role-play, dance, or inventing, while a science test using visual/spatial knowing would involve drawing, painting, active imagination, and sculpting as the primary means by which students demonstrate what they have learned.

4. **Emphasizing children's strengths.** This assessment factor emphasizes giving students the experience of success in school by creating learning activities and lessons that encourage the students to know and learn using their stronger intelligences. Krechevsky suggests that this approach not only increases students' sense of self-esteem, but can spark in them awareness of ways to use their strengths to improve other intelligence areas that are not as strong. I know of few adults who could stand or would tolerate a continual deficit-based assessment of their performance (i.e., "let me tell you all the areas where you are failing!"), and yet we often expect our students to survive twelve years (or more) of these assessments. Why not, instead, ask children who are strong in sports to create a new game about the Bill of Rights? Or have students who love music and rhythm illustrate a story with music and sound? As I mentioned earlier, I believe that we must always remember that anything we have to teach can be taught and learned in a wide variety of ways. We must not be bound by the verbal/linguistic and logical/mathematical prepackaging that controls more than 95 percent of our curriculum materials!

5. **Attending to the stylistic dimensions of performance.** This factor involves carefully tracking how students approach different learning tasks and activities. How do they interact with the material? How do they relate to each other in the midst of a lesson? Project Spectrum is as concerned about students' working styles as with their cognitive skills. In *Seven Ways of Knowing* I suggest allowing students an opportunity to play a variety of intelligence skill–related games, such as Pictionary™, crossword puzzles, Twister™, Name that Tune™, and so on. You can learn a great deal about your students' working styles by carefully observing *how* they approach the game, regardless of the game they have chosen. In the Project Spectrum experiment many students exhibit a great deal of focus, reflection, and skill when they are working in an area in which they feel strong and comfortable.

Conclusion

TRANSFORMING AND RESTRUCTURING THE PLACE CALLED SCHOOL

In *Control Theory in the Classroom,* William Glasser suggests that the most important issue confronting us in American education is that well over 50 percent of the students who inhabit our classrooms day in and day out have absolutely no desire to learn what we are trying to teach them. He suggests further that their lack of interest is not their problem; it is the educators' problem. Until we find a way to make getting an education worth their while, all of our efforts at restructuring curriculum and reforming school policy may be only an interesting diversion.

How do we approach the task of making education worth students' while? How do we increase the payoff now? Glasser notes that there are five basic needs with which every student comes into our classrooms and which all students will find a way to meet in any way they can:

Love: Students want to feel that others love and value them. They need to feel accepted.

Independence: Students want to experience a sense of freedom and independence. They need to feel that they can make decisions on their own.

Fun: Students want and need to enjoy the situation in which they find themselves and will very often go to extreme lengths to create fun if they don't think there is enough fun.

Security: Students need to feel a basic sense that things are right with the world. This need is more difficult to meet, given the lack of stability in many homes today.

Power: Students want to feel in control of what happens to them. They want to have a say in those things that are shaping their lives, even if it is only during a forty-five minute period.

What if we could find ways to meet these five basic needs every day within our classrooms? What if the payoff of education was that these needs were regularly met and fulfilled? Glasser suggests that the percentage of students "on board with their education" would likely be far higher.

One of the main reasons that I am so excited about multiple intelligences is that I believe, and have witnessed in hundreds of schools and districts across North America, that this approach to teaching and learning addresses these basic needs. I have seen students who have experienced failure in their studies for years suddenly experience success. I have seen countless teachers experience a renewed excitement for their chosen profession. I have experienced dramatic shifts in both students' and teachers' levels of self-esteem as they discover ways to affirm their unique ways of knowing and discover that they are not "weird" or "strange" just because they do not excel in verbal/linguistic or logical/ mathematical intelligence capacities. I invite you to join this journey of self-discovery and to likewise invite your students to begin to know themselves intellectually.

Bibliography

Alexander, F. *The Use of the Self: Its Conscious Direction in Relation to Diagnosis, Functioning, and the Control of Reaction.* Downey, Calif.: Centerline Press, 1984.

Ambruster, B., and T. Anderson. *The Effect of Mapping on the Free Recall of Expository Tests.* Tech. Rep. No. 160. Urbana-Champaign, Ill.: University of Illinois, Center for the Study of Reading, 1980.

Anderson, R., and W. Biddle. "On Asking People Questions about What They Are Reading." In G. Brower (ed.), *The Psychology of Learning and Motivation.* New York: Academic Press, 1975.

Arlin, P. "Teaching as Conversation." *Educational Leadership* 48 (2), 1990.

Armstrong, T. *In Their Own Way: Discovering and Encouraging Your Child's Personal Learning Style.* Los Angeles: J. P. Tarcher, 1987.

————. *Seven Kinds of Smart: Identifying and Developing Your Many Intelligences.* New York: Penguin Books, 1993.

Assagioli, R. *The Act of Will.* New York: Viking Press, 1973.

Ausubel, D. *Educational Psychology: A Cognitive View.* New York: Holt, Rinehart, and Winston, 1968.

Bacon, F. "Of Studies." In W. Louis (ed.), *Century Readings in the English Essay.* New York: Appleton-Century-Crofts, 1939.

Bartlett, F. *Thinking.* New York: Basic Books, 1958.

Bellanca, J., and R. Fogarty. *Blueprints for Thinking in the Cooperative Classroom.* Rev. ed. Palatine, Ill.: Skylight Publishing, 1986.

————. *Catch Them Thinking.* Palatine, Ill.: Skylight Publishing, 1991.

Benson, H. *The Relaxation Response.* New York: Morrow, 1975.

Beyer, B. *Practical Strategies for the Teaching of Thinking.* Boston: Allyn & Bacon, 1987.

Bloom, B. *Taxonomy of Educational Objectives.* New York: David McKay, 1956.

Bogen, J. *Some Education Aspects of Hemispheric Socialization.* Pomona, N.Y.: Dromenon, 1979.

Boulding, K. *The Image.* Ann Arbor: University of Michigan Press, 1966.

Bruner, J., J. Goodnow, and G. Austin. *A Study of Thinking*. New York: Wiley, 1956.

Buzan, T. *Use Both Sides of Your Brain*. New York: Dutton, 1991.

Caine, R., and G. Caine. "Understanding a Brain-Based Approach to Learning and Teaching." *Educational Leadership* 48 (2): 66–70, 1990.

Campbell, D. *Introduction to the Musical Brain*. Richardson, Tex.: Magnamusic-Baton, 1983.

Campbell, J. *The Improbable Machine: What the Upheavals in Artificial Intelligence Research Reveal about How the Mind Really Works*. New York: Simon and Schuster, 1989.

Campbell, L. *Tomorrow's Education Today*. Seattle: The Pegasus School, 1985.

Campbell, L., B. Campbell, and D. Dickenson. *Teaching and Learning through Multiple Intelligences*. Seattle: New Horizons for Learning, 1992.

Chomsky, N. *Language and Mind*. New York: Harcourt Brace Jovanovich, 1968.

Churchill, Winston. *My Early Life: A Roving Commission*. New York: Scribner, 1987.

Costa, A. "Mediating the Metacognitive." *Educational Leadership*. 42 (3): 57–62, 1984.

———. "The School as a Home for the Mind." In Costa, *Developing Minds*.

———. "Teaching for Intelligent Behavior." *Educational Leadership* 39 (1): 29–31, 1981.

———. "Thinking Skills: Neither an Add-on nor a Quick Fix." In *Developing Minds*.

Costa, A., ed. *Developing Minds*. Rev. ed. Alexandria, Va.: Association for Supervision and Curriculum Development, 1991.

Culicover, P., and Wexler, P. *Formal Principles of Language Acquisition*. Cambridge, Mass.: MIT Press, 1980.

Curry, L. "A Critique of the Research on Learning Styles." *Educational Leadership* 48 (2): 50–52, 1990.

Dansereai, D., et al. "Development and Evaluation of a Learning Strategy Training Program." *Journal of Educational Psychology* 71 (1): 1979.

Davidson, J. "The Group Mapping Activity for Instruction in Reading and Thinking." *Journal of Reading* 26 (1): 52–56, 1982.

de Bono, E. *Lateral Thinking: Creativity Step by Step*. New York: Harper and Row, 1973.

Dickinson, D. *New Developments in Cognitive Research*. Seattle: New Horizons for Learning, 1987.

Dunne, J. *The Way of all the Earth: Experiments in Truth and Religion*. New York: MacMillan, 1972.

Feldenkrais, M. *Awareness through Movement: Health Exercises for Personal Growth*. New York: Harper and Row, 1977.

Ferguson, M. *The Aquarian Conspiracy: Personal and Social Transformation in the 1980's*. Los Angeles: J. P. Tarcher, 1980.

Feuerstein, R. *Instrumental Enrichment*. Baltimore, Md.: University Park Press, 1980.

Fogarty, R., and J. Bellanca. *Patterns for Thinking: Patterns for Transfer*. Palatine, Ill.: Skylight Publishing, 1989.

———. *Teach Them Thinking*. Palatine, Ill.: Skylight Publishing, 1986.

Gardner, H. "Developing the Spectrum of Human Intelligences: Teaching in the Eighties, a Need to Change." *Harvard Educational Review,* 1987.

———. *Developmental Psychology: An Introduction.* Boston: Little Brown, 1982.

———. "Do Babies Sing a Universal Song?" *Psychology Today,* December 1981.

———. *Frames of Mind: The Theory of Multiple Intelligences.* New York: Harper and Row, 1983.

———. *Multiple Intelligences: The Theory in Practice.* New York: Basic Books, 1993.

———. *The Unschooled Mind: How Children Think and How Schools Should Teach.* New York: Basic Books, 1991.

Gawain, S. *Creative Visualization.* New York: Bantam Books, 1978.

Gazzaniga, M. *Mind Matters: How Mind and Brain Interact to Create Our Conscious Lives.* Boston: Houghton Mifflin, 1988.

Gendlin, E. *Focusing.* New York: Everest House, 1978.

Glasser, W. *Control Theory in the Classroom.* New York: Perennial Library, 1986.

Graham, I. "Mindmapping: An Aid to Memory." In Brian Steinfield (ed.), *Planetary Edges.* Toronto: The Institute of Cultural Affairs, 1988.

Guilford, J. *Way Beyond IQ.* Buffalo, N.Y.: Creative Education Foundation, 1979.

Harman, W. *The Global Mind Change.* Indianapolis: Knowledge Systems, 1988.

Harman, W., and H. Rheingold. *Higher Creativity.* Los Angeles: J. P. Tarcher, 1985.

Hart, Leslie. *Human Brain and Human Learning.* Village of Oak Creek, Ariz.: Books for Educators, 1983.

Houston, J. *Lifeforce: The Psycho-historical Recovery of the Self.* New York: Delacorte Press, 1980.

———. *The Possible Human: A Course in Extending Your Physical, Mental, and Creative Abilities.* Los Angeles: J. P. Tarcher, 1982.

———. *The Search for the Beloved: Journeys in Sacred Psychology.* Los Angeles: J. P. Tarcher, 1987.

Hubbard, B. *Manual for Co-Creators of the Quantum Leap.* Irvine, Calif.: Barbara Marx Hubbard, 1985.

Institute of Cultural Affairs. *5th City Pre-School Education Manual.* Chicago: Institute of Cultural Affairs, 1968.

———. *Imaginal Training Methods. Image: A Journal on the Human Factor.* April–June, 1981

Johnson, D., R. Johnson, and E. J. Holubec. *Circles of Learning.* Edina Minn.: Interaction Book Company, 1986.

———. *Cooperation in the Classroom.* Edina, Minn.: Interaction Book Company, 1988.

Kagan, S. *Cooperative Learning Resources for Teachers.* San Juan Capistrano, Calif.: Resources for Teachers, 1990.

Kazantzakis, N. *The Saviours of God.* New York: Simon and Schuster, 1960.

Laird, C. *The Miracle of Language.* New York: Fawcett Publications, 1957.

Langer, S. *Reflections on Art.* New York: Arno Press, 1979.

Lawrence, D. "Search for Love." In V. de Sola Pinto and F. Roberts (eds). *The Complete Poems of D. H. Lawrence.* New York: Viking Press, 1959.

Lazear, D. *Multiple Intelligence Approach to Assessment: Solving the Assessment Conundrum.* Tucson, Ariz.: Zephyr Press, 1994.

————. *Seven Ways of Knowing: Teaching for Multiple Intelligences.* Palatine, Ill.: Skylight Publishing, 1991a.

————. *Seven Ways of Teaching: The Artistry of Teaching With Multiple Intelligences.* Palatine, Ill.: Skylight Publishing, 1991b.

————. *Teaching for Multiple Intelligences.* Bloomington, Ind.: Phi Delta Kappa, 1992.

Leonard, George. *The Silent Pulse: The Search for the Perfect Rhythm that Exists in Each of Us.* New York: Dutton, 1986.

Loye, D. *The Sphinx and the Rainbow: Brain, Mind, and Future Vision.* Boulder, Colo.: New Science Library, 1983.

Lozonov, G. *Suggestology and Outline of Suggestology.* New York: Gordon & Breach, 1978.

Machado, L. *The Right to be Intelligent.* New York: Pergamon Press, 1980.

MacLean, P. "On the Evolution of Three Mentalities." In S. Arieti and G. Chryanowski (eds.), *New Dimensions in Psychiatry: A World View,* vol. 2. New York: Wiley, 1977.

Markley, O. "Using Depth Intuition in Creative Problem Solving and Strategic Innovation." *Journal of Creative Behavior* 22 (2): 85–100, 1988.

Masters, R., and J. Houston. *Listening to the Body: The Psychophysical Way to Health and Awareness.* New York: Delacorte Press, 1978.

————. *Mindgames.* New York: Delacorte Press, 1972.

McTighe, J. "Teaching for Thinking, of Thinking, and about Thinking." In M. Heiman and J. Slomianko (eds.), *Thinking Skills Instruction: Concepts and Techniques.* Washington, D.C.: National Education Association, 1987.

McTighe, J., and F. Lyman. "Cueing Thinking in the Classroom: The Promise of Theory-Embedded Tools." *Educational Leadership* 45 (7): 18–24, 1988.

Monroe, R. *Far Journeys.* Garden City, N.Y.: Doubleday, 1985.

Nat Hahn, T. *The Miracle of Mindfulness.* N.Y.: Beacon Press, 1988.

O'Conner, J., and J. Seymour. *Introduction to Neurolinguistic Programming.* London: Mandala, 1990.

Orff, C. *The Schulwerk.* M. Murray, trans. New York: Schott Music Corporation, 1978.

Perkins, D. *Knowledge as Design.* Hillsdale, N.J.: Lawrence Erlbaum Associates, 1986.

Piaget, J. *The Psychology of Intelligence.* Totowa, N.J.: Littlefield Adams, 1972.

Pribram, K. *Holonomy and Structure in the Organization of Perception.* Stanford, Calif.: Stanford University Press, 1974.

————. *Languages of the Brain: Experimental Paradoxes and Principles in Neuropsychology.* Englewood Cliffs, N.J.: Prentice-Hall, 1971.

Progoff, I. *At a Journal Workshop: The Basic Text and Guide for Using the Intensive Journal.* New York: Dialogue House Library, 1975.

Rico, G. *Writing the Natural Way: Using Right-Brain Techniques to Release Your Expressive Powers.* Los Angeles: J. P. Tarcher, 1983.

Rosenfield, I. *The Invention of Memory: A New View of the Brain.* New York: Basic Books, 1988.

Russell, P. *The Brain Book.* New York: E. P. Dutton, 1976.

———. *The Global Brain: Speculations on the Evolutionary Leap to Planetary Consciousness.* Los Angeles: J. P. Tarcher, 1983.

Samuels, M., and N. Samuels. *Seeing with the Mind's Eye: The History, Techniques, and Uses of Visualization.* New York: Random House, 1975.

Schmeck, R., ed. *Learning Strategies and Learning Styles.* New York: Plenum Press, 1988.

Shone, R. *Creative Visualization.* New York: Thorson's Publishers, 1984.

Slavin, R. *Cooperative Learning.* New York: Longman, 1983.

Snowman, J. "Learning Tactics and Strategies." In G. Phy and T. Andre (eds.), *Cognitive Instructional Psychology: Components of Classroom Learning.* New York: Academic Press, 1989.

Springer, S., and G. Deutsch. *Left Brain, Right Brain.* New York: W. H. Freeman, 1985.

Steiner, R. *Music in Light of Anthroposophy.* London: Anthroposophical, 1925.

Sternberg, R. *Beyond I. Q.: A Triarchic Theory of Human Intelligence.* New York: Cambridge University Press, 1984.

———. *Intelligence Applied: Understanding and Increasing Your Intellectual Skills.* San Diego: Harcourt Brace Jovanovich, 1986.

Sternberg, R., L. Okagaki, and A. Jackson. "Practical Intelligence for Success in School." *Educational Leadership* 48 (1): 35–39, 1990.

Vaughn, F. *The Inward Arc.* Boulder, Colo.: The New Science Library, 1986.

von Oech, R. *A Kick in the Seat of the Pants: Using Your Explorer, Artist, Judge, and Warrior to be More Creative.* New York: Perennial Library, 1986.

———. *A Whack on the Side of the Head: How to Unlock Your Mind for Innovation.* New York: Warner Books, 1983.

Vygotsky, L. *Thought and Language.* Cambridge, Mass.: MIT Press, 1986.

Walsh, R., and F. Vaughn, eds. *Beyond Ego: Transpersonal Dimensions in Psychology.* Los Angeles: J. P. Tarcher, 1980.

Walters, J., and H. Gardner. *The Development and Education of the Intelligences.* Position paper. Chicago: Spencer Foundation; New York: Carnegie Corporation, 1984.

Weinstein, M., and J. Goodman. *Playfair.* San Luis Obispo, Calif.: Impact, 1980.

Wilber, K. *The Atman Project.* Wheaton, Ill.: Quest Books, 1980.

———. *Eye to Eye: The Quest for the New Paradigm.* Garden City, N.Y.: Anchor Books, 1983.

Index

NOTES

NOTES

NOTES

NOTES

NOTES

NOTES

NOTES

NOTES

NOTES

Multiply your teaching power with these products also by David Lazear

MULTIPLE INTELLIGENCE APPROACHES TO ASSESSMENT
Solving the Assessment Conundrum
by David Lazear
foreword by Grant Wiggins
Grades K–12+

Here are more than 1,000 specific ideas to help you accurately assess students' academic progress. Learn how to create intelligence profiles based on your observations. You'll also find practical prescriptive ideas on how to teach to varying intelligences. Save money with a variety of reproducible assessment tools you can use 1 to 1,000 times!

Document and assess your students' work in the midst of daily classroom activities using 6 practical models.

1039-W . . . $44

INTELLIGENCE BUILDERS FOR EVERY STUDENT
44 Exercises to Expand MI in Your Classroom
by David Lazear
Grades 4–8

You'll find these activities excellent for self-discovery and developing classroom cohesiveness. Use this handy resource to build kinesthetic body awareness, linguistic humor, mathematical skills, group dynamics, and more!

1086-W . . . $25

MI IN ACTION
Your School and the Multiple Intelligences
in collaboration with David Lazear
Staff Development

Put these information-packed videos to work for you! Train the key players in your school about the basics of MI, then equip them with the complete set to give others an easy-to-understand overview. You'll be introduced to MI by leading experts: David Lazear, Nancy Margulies, Don Campbell, Anne Bruetsch, and others. You'll get these 5 videos—

1. **Getting the Picture: An Overview**
2. **A Creative Art: Teaching MI in the Elementary Grades**
3. **Tuning in the Learner: MI in Middle and High School Grades**
4. **Testing for Success: MI Assessment**
5. **Miss Ballou, Where Are You? An MI Guide for Parents**

Five 20-minute, full-color, VHS videotapes, and five 8–10 page accompanying booklets.

1705-W . . . $399

Get started with MI— it's easy with these handy resources!

TAP YOUR MULTIPLE INTELLIGENCES
Posters for the Classroom
text by David Lazear
illustrations by Nancy Margulies
Grades 3–12

Help your students use all their intelligences with full-size color posters. This handy set of 8 colorful posters will remind your students to use all 7 intelligences plus explore Howard Gardner's newest addition—the naturalist!

8 full-color posters, printed on lightweight poster board, each one 11" x 17".

1811-W . . . $25

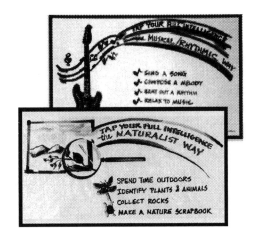

STEP BEYOND YOUR LIMITS
Expanding Your MI Capacities
by David Lazear
Professional Development

Gain valuable insights and nurture your intelligences with a powerful learning tool designed for your development. Start by listening to a 40-minute tape packed with experiential activities and tips for awakening your MI capacities. Each tape has an accompanying workbook that leads you on a self-guided, step-by-step, capacity-building and enhancement program. The workbooks contain carefully designed exercises for helping you fully develop the distinct capacities related to each intelligence.

Eight 40-minute audiotapes and 7 workbooks: One tape on each intelligence and one overview tape; one workbook for each intelligence.

1914-W . . . $175

ORDER FORM ☎ Please include your phone number in case we have questions about your order.

Qty.	Item #	Title	Unit Price	Total
	1039-W	Multiple Intelligence Approaches to Assessment	$44	
	1086-W	Intelligence Builders for Every Student	$25	
	1705-W	MI in Action	$399	
	1811-W	Tap Your Multiple Intelligences	$25	
	1914-W	Step Beyond Your Limits	$175	

Name _____

Address _____

City _____

State _____ Zip _____

Phone (_____) _____

Method of payment (check one):

❏ Check or Money Order ❏ Visa

❏ MasterCard ❏ Purchase Order Attached

Credit Card No. _____

Expires _____

Signature _____

Subtotal	
Sales Tax (AZ residents, 5%)	
S & H (10% of Subtotal, min.$3.00)	
Total (U.S. Funds only)	

CANADA: add 22% for S& H and G.S.T.

100% SATISFACTION GUARANTEE

Upon receiving your order you'll have 90 days of risk-free evaluation. If you are not 100% satisfied, return your order in saleable condition within 90 days for a 100% refund of the purchase price.

CALL, WRITE, OR FAX FOR YOUR FREE CATALOG!

To order write or call:

Zephyr Press ®

REACHING THEIR HIGHEST POTENTIAL

P.O. Box 66006-W
Tucson, AZ 85728-6006

(520) 322-5090
FAX (520) 323-9402